Dearest Graham

You are quite simply ~~ —
I laughed out loud when
reading this book — hope it
does the same with you!
                    Chitra xxx

SECOND-CLASS MALE

SECOND-CLASS MALE

A BOOK OF
MISGUIDED LETTERS

STAN MADELEY

Michael O'Mara Books Limited

First published in Great Britain in 2010 by
Michael O'Mara Books Limited
9 Lion Yard
Tremadoc Road
London SW4 7NQ

Copyright © Stanley Madeley 2010

Every reasonable effort has been made to acknowledge all copyright holders. Any errors or omissions that may have occurred are inadvertent, and anyone with any copyright queries is invited to write to the publishers, so that a full acknowledgement may be included in subsequent editions of this work.

All rights reserved. No part of this publication may be reproduced, stored in a retrieval system, or transmitted by any means, without the prior permission in writing of the publisher, nor be otherwise circulated in any form of binding or cover other than that in which it is published and without a similar condition including this condition being imposed on the subsequent purchaser.

A CIP catalogue record for this book is available from the British Library.

Papers used by Michael O'Mara Books Limited are natural, recyclable products made from wood grown in sustainable forests. The manufacturing processes conform to the environmental regulations of the country of origin.

ISBN: 978-1-84317-491-2

1 3 5 7 9 10 8 6 4 2

Cover design by Sandra Madeley (54)
Typesetting by www.blokgraphic.com
Photo of Rudyard on p78 courtesy of the Library of Congress, Bain Collection, LC-B2-773-13

Printed and bound in Great Britain by Clays Ltd, St Ives plc

www.mombooks.com

To Richard Madeley
(the UK's top Stan Madeley lookalike)

STAN MADELEY
THE UK'S TOP RICHARD MADELEY LOOKALIKE
BM NOUMENON, LONDON, WC1N 3XX   EMAIL: STAN@STANMADELEY.COM

Mr. Michael O'Mara
Michael O'Mara Books
16 Lion Yard
Tremadoc Road
London, SW4 7NQ

1st January, 2010

Dear Michael,

Do you believe in fate? Kismet? The music of the spheres? No, neither do I. It's bull-rot for the masses. But I do believe that like-minded men should work together, bare-chested if the need arises. And there's no shame in that. Is there?

Allow me to introduce myself. The name is Stanley Madeley (by deed poll) and I'm the UK's top Richard Madeley lookalike, as well as a regular fixture on the nation's cabaret circuit. If you have any love for the Alpine horn, you'll probably have seen my surrealist one-man show, 'Flagrant Heron Abuse – The Stanley Madeley Experience Live!'. And up to six months ago, I was also the country's only chisel-throwing act licensed to perform before children.

But let me get down to business. The other afternoon, I was buttering my heels in the local Waterstone's whilst wife, Sandra (54), was across the road in Boots returning a pair of faulty birthing stirrups. That's when I found myself thumbing through one of your publications. Can't remember the title. I think it had a goat on the cover. But I was impressed by what I saw. Heavy paper, nicely bound, whacking big price tag on the back: undoubtedly a quality product. Anyway, I quickly jotted down your name on the corner of a page that I quietly ripped off and pocketed among the celebrity biographies. You see, I have a proposition for you, Michael.

It boils down to this: I'm looking for a publisher for my new book. Currently, the title stands at: *Second-Class Male: The Unpublished Correspondence of the UK's Top Richard Madeley Lookalike*, though I'm open to suggestions, especially if I can get the word 'shite' up top in a big font. If it works for the other books you publish, I'd like it to work for mine. It also gives me very great pride to offer this book to the publisher who printed the great Willie Donaldson's *Soap Letters*. It's win/win all down the line.

I realise, of course, that we need some star names to bring in the punters, so what if I offer to throw in replies from Alan Bennett, The Bishop of Liverpool, Quentin Letts, Sir David Attenborough, Terry Gilliam, Mathew Parris, John Prescott, Brian Sewell, Black Rod, Mr. Kipling, Daniel Corbett, The British Flute Society, Terry Wogan, The National Portrait Gallery, The Joint Commission of Biochemical Nomclemature, Derren Brown, The League Against Cruel Sports, some nuns, as well as a terse email response from Su Pollard's assistant? There are many

STAN MADELEY
THE UK'S TOP RICHARD MADELEY LOOKALIKE
BM NOUMENON, LONDON, WC1N 3XX   EMAIL: STAN@STANMADELEY.COM

others with more arriving with each post, though Colonel Gaddafi has yet to get back to me via letter or henchman.

Let me be perfectly blunt with you, Michael. I'm not going to drag this around London hoping to find an agent with a sense of humour. I mean: do I look that crazy? (Signed glossy publicity photo enclosed.) No, I'm writing only to you because you understand a belly laugh.

You're probably wondering if this deal sounds too good to be true. Well, I'm not claiming originality but I do have a face fit for hardback and I'm a damn sight funnier than some of the chancers bending your arm for a book deal. However, it's your reputation as a hard-as-nails editor who doesn't put up with fools that impresses me the most. As a hard-as-nails cabaret star, I suggest we get drunk and settle percentages whilst bareknuckling our way through London's pubs. What do you say to that? We'd be like *The Quiet Man* but without the bonnets or Maureen O'Hara.

Your friend in cabaret,

[signature]

> Sandra, my literary career begins here... Now pencil me in for new teeth and a fatwa.

STAN MADELEY
THE UK'S TOP RICHARD MADELEY LOOKALIKE
BM NOUMENON, LONDON, WC1N 3XX   EMAIL: STAN@STANMADELEY.COM

Mr. Steve Pound MP
House of Commons
London SW1A 0AA

1st February, 2010

Dear Steve,

Or is it Stephen? One finds it so hard to tell which. On your blog, you're a Steve. Yet on TV, you're a Stephen. 'Steve' makes you appear more of the people but 'Stephen' sounds more dignified. Not that I suppose it matters much. I was chin to rubber Yoga mat a week or two ago, inverted in the Sirsasana position, when I found myself listening to you on Sky News. By the time you'd finished, there was quite the grin on my face, though my wife Sandra (54), thought I was frowning. The reason for my inverted cheerfulness was that you mentioned that you enjoy getting correspondence via letter rather than email. I couldn't agree more. Giddy at the news and with the blood still rushing from my ears, I immediately sat down to start composing this letter.

Well, it may have taken me a fortnight but I've finally found something to say. You see, I'm not a political man, Steve. Cabaret is my gig of choice. I make a comfortable living travelling the country as the UK's top (and only) Richard Madeley lookalike. It means I carry out most of my correspondence by letter. I stand toe to toe with the postal service, Steve. It's the lifeblood of the country. I was wondering, therefore, if you'd say a few words in the Big House or on TV in favour of UK letter writers?

The fact is there's something so reassuring about opening an envelope and finding a quality sheet of the Conqueror bonded inside. That's why I firmly believe in replying to correspondence and would like to shame those that don't. If you need it, I have a long list of people, companies, and government bodies who don't demonstrate even an ounce of basic civility by replying. On the other hand, I also have a list of people who exceed all expectations. For example, Quentin Letts at the *Daily Mail* is the Ghandi of correspondents. You can't squeak out a sneeze within earshot of him without receiving a 'thank you' in the morning post. Compare his example with that of that villain Simon Hoggart at *The Guardian*. Too busy to bother penning a decent reply, even when the postage is paid up front.

The point is, Steve/Stephen: if more of us wrote letters, the Post Office wouldn't be in such a mess. And if the recipients of the letters bothered to send a reply, we'd find it hard to import enough highly trained university lecturers from Russia to deliver our mail. This is basic economics and I think as an MP you're in a position to give the British economy the kick in the shins that it needs.

Your friend in cabaret,

PS. Where do you buy your ties? My wife, Sandra (54), thinks you have some of the sharpest neckwear in the business and that includes Theresa May's scarves!

STEPHEN POUND MP

HOUSE OF COMMONS
LONDON SW1A 0AA

Stan Madeley
B M Noumenon
London
WC1N 3XX

10 February 2010

My Ref: MADE01001

Dear Stan Madeley,

Thank you very much indeed for your letter of 1 February and I hope you will forgive me for saying that never again will I be able to expose myself to the nation on Sky News without thinking of you inverted on the yoga mat.

I hope you will also forgive me for saying that during the course of a long life and, having knocked around a bit in some of the more louche quarters of the metropolis, I have never ever had the honour to make the acquaintance of the official Richard Madeley look-alike.

I did appear on the Richard and Judy Show on a few occasions and was gratified to be presented with a bottle of champagne that all guests receive. In the more relaxed regimen that prevailed at that time I felt no need to declare the emolument particularly as I always presented it to the Big Issue seller on Westminster Bridge.

My innate politeness causes me to refrain from asking if your wife Sandra (54) bears any resemblance to Judith Finnigan. If this is the case, might I gently suggest that she has the best of the bargain.

I also have some difficulty with your description of Quentin Letts as the Ghandi of correspondence, I rather like Quentin and have a signed copy of his *'50 people who buggered up Britain'* before me on my desk as I write. However, I never saw anything that linked him with the selfless aestheticism of the Mahatma although I never went out on the lash with M K Ghandi as he was assassinated in 1948 before I was born, I have however enjoyed Quentin's company on occasion and he would have no objection to my confirming that he does not subsist on an alcohol free pure vegetarian diet.

Contd./......

STEPHEN POUND MP

I entirely agree with your point concerning the beauties of the epistolatory art and continue to send out several hundred letters every week although few of them are in response to one as original and charming to that which you kindly sent me.

My very best wishes to both you and Sandra (54).

Yours sincerely,

STEPHEN POUND
MP for Ealing North

What a lovely chap! Sandra, put him on the Christmas list instead of Michael Gove.

1 lb of tapioca + sprouts

STAN MADELEY
THE UK'S TOP RICHARD MADELEY LOOKALIKE
BM NOUMENON, LONDON, WC1N 3XX EMAIL: STAN@STANMADELEY.COM

Alan Bennett
c/o Charles Walker
United Agents
London, W1F 0LE

4th September, 2009

Dear Mr. Bennett (or representative of Mr. Bennett, of whom I most humbly beg the favour of 'passing this on'),

Allow me to introduce myself. My name is Stanley Madeley (by deed poll) and I am the UK's top Richard Madeley lookalike. You might recognise me from the cabaret circuit which I've worked for the last fifteen years with my wife Sandra (54). I am writing, however, as a fan. I have read all your books and plays and you are the man who has most inspired and influenced my writing. My letter to 'Practical Goldfish' recently netted me (pun intended) £2! I have you to thank for that and enclose a book token for half that amount. I trust you will put it to good use.

It would make me the proudest member of the East Hackney Writer's Circle if you could be so good as to read this example of my dialogue and tell me if you think it's lacking in punctuation. I have been writing the play (titled 'Shropshire Fop') for nearly six years and this part has given me the most trouble:

> **SERF:** Your Lordship! It's the onion seller! I recognise him! He's the man I saw tangled upon Lady Penelope's trellis t'other night.
>
> **SIR HENRY:** Ah ha! He is, is he? Then he shall weep at the sting of more than a few ripe shallots. Pass me my blade so I can enscribble mine moniker upon his liquorice hide!
>
> **SERF:** But beware, Sire. His pantaloons bulge awkwardly. I suspect a flintlock down his hose.
>
> **SIR HENRY:** Methinks he has cause for cowardice! No man dare look Sir Henry Witherspoon in the monocle and not tremble about the knee! Out of my way so I might puncture him with my viperfish dagger.

When you're done, I wonder if I could also press you for a signed photograph. Mrs. Peel, my writing teacher, doesn't think you'll reply, but what does she know? Since her hysterectomy she's started to shave regularly and loses her temper at Mrs. Small's poodle, Shirley Saffron III.

As an extra incentive, I have included my own signed glossy as tribute to you and yours. I only hope you will treasure it above hearth or mantle.

Kindest wishes,

STAN MADELEY
THE UK'S TOP RICHARD MADELEY LOOKALIKE
BM NOUMENON, LONDON, WC1N 3XX   EMAIL: STAN@STANMADELEY.COM

Mr. Alan Bennett   9th December, 2009

Dearest Alan,

Given that I'm younger, more working class, and far less menopausal than your usual audience, I hope I might be forgiven the vulgar, presumptuous manner by which I have addressed this letter to your home. My wife, Sandra (54), had threatened to start divorce proceedings if I didn't write. You see, she has been constantly berating me these last few months for falling into a state of profound melancholy. The reason for my depression: a letter I sent to you, via your agent, on the 4th September, 2009.

That you didn't reply has given me no end of restless nights and I am now forced to sleep outside in the campervan (sans duvet). The thought that I might have annoyed one of my literary heroes has distressed me enormously. My nails are bitten so far to the knuckle that I've even had occasion to taste elbow.

Yet this morning I still took your *Untold Stories* down from the shelf. It's something of a 'regular' habit (excuse the soon-to-develop pun) that I read your diaries whilst undertaking my morning ablutions. I usually find the timing of one 'entry' just right for one 'exit', so to speak. However, due to some questionably-sourced chicken with last night's roast spud, this morning's reading session was longer than usual and I managed to reach page 301 three days ahead of schedule. That's where you write (10 December): 'I always acknowledge letters, though seldom pursue a correspondence'. As you can imagine, by this point my legs were fairly numb, my knees as cold as porcelain, but I still managed to rush downstairs and present this evidence to my wife. Unbeknownst to me, Sandra (54) was in the process of writing out a cheque towards the local church's Christmas fund so my appearance in the living room 'unzippered to the bells', as they say, came as something of a surprise to the vicar, who promptly quoted from the Book of Isaiah: 'Thy nakedness shall be uncovered, yea, thy shame shall be seen'. I thought he did quite well considering the circumstances.

Nevertheless, I'm not a man to doubt another as to the handling of his correspondence. If you say you 'always acknowledge letters', then I believe that you do – though I bet you have some right chancers, dullards, blow-broths, and nincompoops writing to you! I also fear that the £1 book token I sent you is lost, no doubt tucked down the blouse of some secretarial type working for your agent. I was hoping you'd spend it on a volume of Larkin's best but suspect it's gone towards some dreadful ecumenical on the Church of Celebrity.

Anyway, what interest would you have in an aging Northern cabaret performer with a chisel-throwing act that earns him rave reviews? The *Warrington Guardian* described my stage show as 'unique', 'misjudged' and 'requiring further investigation by authorities everywhere'. I suppose I should have the good grace to accept such praise and my place in society's B-list.

      Your friend in cabaret,

      Stan Madeley

PS. Is there any remote chance you'd allow me to park my campervan in your garden?

YD 01 Malham Cove
© Yan Preston

December 19'09

My conscience is clear. I never got your letter at the book token, probably because my agent, now United Agents, split off from PFD where your letter presumably still sits. They don't forward letters despite taking 10% of my earnings still which, hmph, I don't like to think of it.

Do you know that... goes into the pockets of Andrew Neil.

Malham Cove may have been formed 50,000 years ago, and it is 70 meters (230 ft) high!

www.yorkshiredale.org.uk
www.yanoutdoor.com, sales@yanoutdoor.com

YORKSHIRE DALES
National Park

You don't look like Richard Madeley at all for which you should be grateful.

I normally do a better portrait than this but I've run out due to Christmas. I'm sorry to have kept you in suspense for so long. But thank you & I'm glad you enjoy.

U.S.
wherever
to read Alex Janes

YANOUTDOOR Photography

14

STAN MADELEY
THE UK'S TOP RICHARD MADELEY LOOKALIKE
BM NOUMENON, LONDON, WC1N 3XX   EMAIL: STAN@STANMADELEY.COM

Mr. Alan Bennett   24th December, 2009

Dear Alan,

Thank you so much for your kind words, which arrived this morning. And on Christmas Eve, no less, so forgive me if I'm slightly tipsy on the mulled wine or if my finger occasionally gets stuck under the CAPS LOCK key!

I would not normally trouble you with a reply but your postcard gave me so much pleasure that I thought it worth gifting you a little something back in the way of encouragement. I sensed that you sounded a little jaded as to your relationship with your agents and I didn't want you to worry. They may have pocketed the book voucher I sent you and it certainly fills me with no pleasure to think that it might have landed in Andrew Neil's pocket. However, I'll now write to the top people at Waterstone's to see if they have a record of his cashing it in. If this doesn't end in the High Court, my name isn't Stan Madeley!

I would also direct a letter to Andrew Neil himself but he never has the courtesy to reply, even when a man writes to commend him on his Byronic sideburns circa Messolonghi, 1824. I suggest that he's too busy with the dozen jobs he currently holds and the dozen incomes he keeps from a dozen families. Though if I'd known he had such power within publishing circles, I might have held back on the slightly ribald letters I have been sending his way. I'll never land an agent now as I've clearly burned far too many bridges in that well-coiffured Caledonian direction.

No need to apologise for the postcard. I'm from the Lancashire side of those hills and find them just as spiritually uplifting. I can also see that you've adopted the form of the postcard masterfully. They convey a personal touch yet impose a word limit that must be a boon to a man of limited time and patience. It's a clever ruse and I commend your approach. I might even adopt it myself when the letters from Mr. Neil's solicitors start to pattern my doormat in shades of libel.

Your friend in cabaret,

Stan Madeley

> Sandra, this silence can only mean he's writing a part for you. Don't shave your legs until you hear from him.

STAN MADELEY
THE UK'S TOP RICHARD MADELEY LOOKALIKE
BM NOUMENON, LONDON, WC1N 3XX EMAIL: STAN@STANMADELEY.COM

Mr. Gerry Johnson
Waterstone's Booksellers Ltd
Capital Court,
Capital Interchange Way

26th December, 2009

Dear Gerry,

I should imagine that it's rare that you receive letters from talent, so to speak. Your job is very much that of the monkey, collecting brass whilst the organ grinder produces his sweet melody. But allow me to stop grinding my organ a moment to introduce myself. The name is Stanley Madeley (by deed poll) and I am the UK's top Richard Madeley lookalike, as well as being a staple of the British cabaret circuit with my one-man show, 'Knee High Spading – The Stanley Madeley Experience Live!'.

I am writing to you on a matter of some urgency. As you will have noticed, it was recently Christmas. I trust you had a fine one, enjoyed by family and all. Mine was ruined by some shocking news. Like many men with a wide collection of friends in the entertainment field, I shop early for Christmas. That's why I visited one of your stores back in October to purchase a book token which I subsequently sent to my good friend Mr. Alan Bennett, the noted playwright and postcard collector. However, he informed me on Christmas Eve that the book token did not arrive and we now suspect that it has been intercepted en route. I am writing to ask if you know of any way that we might establish if the token has been 'cashed in' and, if so, would it be possible to inspect the CCTV footage of your stores during this period?

We suspect that the man handing in the token would be of Caledonian descent with an elevated forehead. He would be sporting Byronic sideburns and would be in a very great rush due to his having many business commitments around the city. However, he might have loitered if any of your staff or patrons had revealed a shapely ankle. If you have a facility to observe him in the infra-red, he would show up as a rather hot heat signature.

I enclose an artist's impression of the man in question, though the artist in question is my wife Sandra (54) and her impressions were very much dictated by the seasonal grape stewed, mulled, and then given ample throat. She also has a habit of including moustaches where no moustache exists.

If you've seen this man and know what he might have done with my book token, I'd been extremely grateful if you could tip me the wink.

    I remain, a loyal patron of your stores,

Still no reply, Sandra? It's a conspiracy! Mr. Neil has some powerful friends. You'll have to start the car for me each morning.

17

STAN MADELEY
THE UK'S TOP RICHARD MADELEY LOOKALIKE
BM NOUMENON, LONDON, WC1N 3XX   EMAIL: STAN@STANMADELEY.COM

Sir Ian McKellen
Theatre Royal Haymarket
Haymarket,
London, SW1Y 4HT

8th February, 2010

Dear Ian,

The two of us go so far back (1963) that I feel like I don't need to put on any airs and graces. Delighted, of course, when you were elevated by HM the Q but I never forget that we both started out at the bottom. It's just a shame that my discipline (cabaret) hasn't had the same pull among the toffs as Shakespeare and Beckett. But I suppose that's what happens when you only get to carry Coriolanus' spear as a lad!

Anyway, I've carved out a niche for myself as Stanley Madeley (by deed poll), the UK's top Richard Madeley lookalike. So if you ever fancy a night's entertainment (spoon magic, balloon bending, trouser ventriloquism) you should not hesitate to give me a call.

However, that's not the reason I'm reconnecting with you after such a long time. I've just read your comments regarding the Government's new anti-paedophile database. You argue that the rules will prevent theatres from using child actors.

Well, what's wrong with that? Surely you're still not convinced that there's a need for child actors! Is there anything certain to set your teeth on edge than some snotty little nine year-old with the confidence of a well-ripened Vanessa Feltz? And there's nothing that a child actor does that can't equally be done by a short adult. (You know, of course, that I say 'short adult' when I really mean nanus, midget, or munchkin. But I think 'short adult' is a better way of saying it.)

Personally, I'd only use child actors for stunt work too dangerous for an adult or for any production where there's a cap on salaries and cheap labour a necessity. I'm afraid, therefore, on this one matter my sympathies are with the government.

Not that I'm condemning you too much. You always had a kind heart and I still remember fondly that day that you picked up my spear when I dropped it during a matinee performance.

By the way: my wife, Sandra (54), sends you her love. She remembers you well from our days at the Nottingham Playhouse. You might recall that she was a rigger. Spent most of her time sneaking up into the gods to enjoy a covert cigarette. Happier days, I'm sure you'll agree ...

Your old friend in cabaret,

Ian McKellen

Stan Madeley
BM Moumenon
London WC1N 3XX

23 February 2010

Dear Stan Madeley

Thank you very much for your letter after all these years – you are looking good.

As an ex-child actor myself (strictly amateur), I'm trying not to take offence at your remarks. Mind you I am working with three kids in WAITING FOR GODOT and still trying to work out which of them I like least.

all best wishes

Ian McK.

STAN MADELEY
THE UK'S TOP RICHARD MADELEY LOOKALIKE
BM NOUMENON, LONDON, WC1N 3XX   EMAIL: STAN@STANMADELEY.COM

Arriva Trains
(Newport Lost Property Office)
Newport Train Station
Queensway, Newport

25th November, 2009

Dear Sir/Madam,

I recently travelled on your Chester to Manchester Piccadilly service which arrived in Manchester around 8.15AM on 20/11/09. I was travelling with a group of friends – we are touring vaudevillians – and I believe we left an item of luggage on the train.

This would not have mattered so much had we not been the cast of the well-reviewed cabaret show 'The Stanley Madeley Experience Live!' as the items contained in the bag form an important part of our coming festive extravaganza. I am, by the way, THE Stanley Madeley (by deed poll) and, given my reputation as the UK's top Richard Madeley lookalike, I am eager that the items are returned as quickly as possible.

The bag is a large Samsonite case, hard-backed, of a grey colour and with a large sticker of the Swiss flag on the top. The case contained the following:

- Three gold lame swimming costumes
- A pair of inflatable water-wings
- A collapsible stovepipe hat (black)
- A roll of double-backed thong adhesive
- A map of North Korea with annotations in a careful hand
- A folded wall-chart detailing differences between a munchkin and a midget
- A selection of unctions and balms used by Mr. C.C. Potter, our escapologist
- A terrapin skin wallet containing roubles and unused prophylactics
- A bottle of cheap rubbing alcohol which had been only half drunk
- A signed copy of *Just Biggins* (hardcover) by Mr. Christopher Biggins
- Two glass eyeballs (one blue, the other brown)
- A short knife used for the purposes of sword swallowing by Wee Pickens, our tour nanus
- A Bible containing a signed photo of Ms. Fiona Bruce

If you know the whereabouts of the case or perhaps have it in storage in your facility, I would be enormously grateful if you could engineer its safe return.

Finally, can I commend yourself and all the staff at Arriva Trains. The guard on duty was extremely helpful when it came to locating Mr. Potter when he got trapped in the onboard (in)convenience.

Faithfully yours,

Stan Madeley

Stanley Madeley, Owner & Ringmaster, The Stanley Madeley Experience Live

ARRIVA

Lost Property Office
Arriva Trains Wales
Newport Railway Station
Queensway
Newport

Customer Relations Tel No: - 0845 6061 660

11th December 09

Dear Mr Madeley

Thank you, for your letter enquiring after your lost item. After a detailed search at the Lost Property Office I am sorry to inform you that your suitcase has not been handed in to Arriva Trains Wales.

I really enjoyed reading your letter it gave me a few laughs and brightened my day. I will keep your letter on file and will let you know if it turns up. Please try the number below in your quest of tracing the suitcase.

Please contact Manchester LPO on: - 01612 368667

I am sorry I could not be of any more assistance to you in tracking down your item.

Kind Regards

Gillian Miles
LPO Administrator

Arriva Trains Wales Limited
Registered in England and Wales Number 04337645
Registered Office Brunel House,
2 Fitzalan Road, Cardiff CF24 0SU

Trenau Arriva Cymru Cyfyngedig
Cofrestrwyd yn Lloegr a Chymru Rhif 04337645
Swyddfa Gofrestredig Tŷ Brunel,
2 Ffordd Fitzalan, Caerdydd CF24 0SU

STAN MADELEY
THE UK'S TOP RICHARD MADELEY LOOKALIKE
BM NOUMENON, LONDON, WC1N 3XX   EMAIL: STAN@STANMADELEY.COM

Adjustamatic Beds Ltd　　　　　　　　　　　　　　28th September, 2009
Head Office
43/49 High Street
Horley, RH6 7RJ

My dear Sir/Madam,

Allow me to introduce myself. My name is Stanley Madeley (by deed poll) and I am the UK's top Richard Madeley lookalike with my own touring cabaret show, 'Monstrous Gravy Lip – The Stanley Madeley Experience Live!'.

As you can imagine, I am a man who enjoys a good night's sleep. After an evening spent bending spoons, juggling and singing my own brand of ribald song, I need my rest. I was hugely impressed, therefore, when I saw a TV ad recently in which Gloria Hunniford was reclined on an adjustable bed and enjoying the pleasures of a cyclo-massage. Not only is she a fine-looking woman who reminds me, in many ways, of my good wife, Sandra (54), but I believed all her 'honeyed' words. I went out the next day and bought myself a top-of-the-line Adjustamatic double bed with cyclo-massage.

And, can I say, my experiences with the bed have been superb and not a little risqué! I've not known sleeps or adventures quite like the sleeps and adventures I've had in my Adjustamatic bed, and you can quote me on that. My wife, Sandra (54), is also impressed and has recommended your product to her friends. She says the bounce is remarkable and she can achieve a good foot of elevation when she's in sporting mode. However, I thought it important to bring a design flaw to your attention as it ruins what is otherwise a top-quality product. Put simply: there's nowhere to attach the handcuffs.

Oh, you might be saying to yourself, it's *another* of those crank letters. But not so! My wife suffers from acute noctambulism, which to you and me is severe sleepwalking. In the past it has proven extremely dangerous and hard to control. She has broken wrists, ankles, teeth, and legs (not all at the same time) due to her night-time wanderings and she once made it as far as the road outside the local off-licence before she was picked up by a passing Panda car. She has tried sleeping tablets, acupuncture, medication, and hypnosis to cure her of this problem but we've discovered that the best solution is to handcuff her to the bed last thing at night. Unfortunately, with the Adjustamatic bed, I can find no point by which I can confidently secure my wife. We've had to compromise using a length of chain stretched out to the wardrobe handle but this is hardly a long-term solution.

Might I simply suggest that you provide a strong tether point somewhere about the frame? Again, I'd like to repeat: there's nothing 'provincial' about our interest in handcuffs. The purpose of this enquiry is entirely medical, if not an issue of health and safety.

　　　　　　Kind regards,

To: stan@stanmadeley.com
From: Tim Savage <████████████████████>
Date: 05/10/2009 16:33
Subject: Adjustamatic Beds

Dear Stan,

How wonderful to receive your recent communication about your Adjustamatic Bed. Our medical research shows that our beds can aid a good nights sleep and indeed that the cyclo-massage is beneficial at helping with a variety of common medical ailments, it's such a shame that we have, as yet, been unable to help with your dear and rather exotic (by your comments) wife with her sleep patterns. I am however very pleased to read that you have both enjoyed significant "sleeps and adventures" in our lovely bed.

The brief for our new mattress design was very specific in that we really did ask for more "bounce" which is exactly what we achieved to your joint satisfaction no doubt.

I think I may have a solution to the perceived design flaw you mention, although I must admit we have not encountered such an exciting challenge to our R&D department since a much loved elderly couple, who both bought a single bed each, asked us to solve the problem of slipping between their mattress' whilst attempting some of their own nocturnal activity.

I can imagine, and believe me I have, that you wish to keep your dear wife as close as possible during your recumbent hours and that her acute noctambulism must be a constant source of worry, which in turn will reduce your ability to rest and relax whilst enjoying our cyclo-massage. Particularly so after a tough night doing cabaret in the South East.

We have a range of accessories that can be attached to our beds and one of these is known as a "grab" handle, not as exciting as it's name may suggest, it nonetheless does the "job" splendidly. This "u" shaped bracket can be screwed, if you will pardon the expression, to your bed and you can than shackle your wife as snugly as current laws allow.

I have many trained engineers who would be delighted to visit you and your wife to show where we would recommend this be fitted. Before I arrange a visit, can you advise me how long the chain is that connects the handcuffs so we can make the exact size for you.

Your penultimate paragraph dwells on "medical and health and safety issues", rightly so if you want my opinion. I cannot imagine anything worse than trying to sleep knowing that your wife is not shackled to your bed as she should be. Poor you.

If you have any preference in "grab" handle colour or finish we can help here too.

Finally Stan, your likeness to the real Richard Madeley in uncanny, just a little more hair and you are he! If I was you I'd keep clear of Judy as you look much younger and fitter than the real Richard Madeley and allegedly she feels like a new man……….having said that she looks like one too.

Kind regards.

Tim Savage

Group Sales Director

STAN MADELEY
THE UK'S TOP RICHARD MADELEY LOOKALIKE
BM NOUMENON, LONDON, WC1N 3XX   EMAIL: STAN@STANMADELEY.COM

Baroness Boothroyd of Sandwell						8th February, 2010
The House of Lords
London, SW1A 0PW

Dear Betty,

I think I can say, without risk of flattering you too much, that you have always been my favourite Speaker of the House of Commons and the best-looking to boot! Nobody has looked as good in the ceremonial stockings, though, I confess, I have yet to see Mr. Bercow's ankles. Rumour has it that his shins are shapely but they also said that he'd do his utmost to stamp out parliamentary slush funds and look how that's turned out.

Anyway, forgive my writing to you directly and on my professional bonded paper but I have an urgent matter of business to discuss. To quickly gloss over the details: my name is Stanley Madeley (by deed poll) and in addition to my duties as the UK's top Richard Madeley lookalike, I am also a regular fixture on the cabaret stage.

I am in the process of launching my own updated version of the Tiller Girls which I will be naming 'The Stan Madeley Dancers'. Our tag line is 'In it for the kicks!' which should quickly make you realise why I'm writing to you. In this, there can be nobody more suited to answering my question.

You see, to keep the operating costs as low as possible, I've imported two dozen lithe young things from Poland who I've instructed in the art of high kicking whilst linking their arms in formation. We pay for their board and keep and the girls learn a profession. My wife and I plan to bus them around the country to high-quality venues where they will be an added attraction on our already glittering variety bill. We hope to recreate the world of 1950s variety all over again but without all the Ronnies and Reggies.

Things have been going smoothly but I have now run into a small spot of trouble regarding government regulations. I am led to believe that there are national requirements that a Tiller line be no more than 40% Polish (or, indeed, any other foreign nationality). I have contacted various government departments but they have given me no reasonable guidelines. I thought that you might have heard of this ruling or know somebody inside government who could clarify the legal position.

Currently, my Tiller line is entirely Polish, except for my wife Sandra (54 but still with the legs of a 25-year-old) who is herself Luton-born but 25% Romany on her father's side.

I hope you don't think this business too trifling to concern you. I meant what I said about your legs.

			Your friend in cabaret,

The Right Honourable Baroness Boothroyd O.M., P.C.

House of Lords
London SW1A 0PW

15th March 2010

Dear Mr Madeley,

I have your letter dated the 8th February and apologise for not responding earlier, but I have been overseas for some weeks.

Regrettably I cannot assist with your query. Commonsense tells me there cannot be government regulations about the nationality of a Tiller line. Your best method of approach is to return to whoever led you "to believe that there are national restrictions……" and pursue the matter with them.

Thank you for your courtesy in enclosing a stamped addressed envelope/

Yours sincerely,

Betty Boothroyd

Mr. Stanley Madeley,
BM Noumenon,
London, WC1N 3XX

STAN MADELEY
THE UK'S TOP RICHARD MADELEY LOOKALIKE
BM NOUMENON, LONDON, WC1N 3XX   EMAIL: STAN@STANMADELEY.COM

Su Pollard c/o
Liverpool Empire
Liverpool, L1 1JE

8th November, 2009

My dear Su,

Allow me to introduce myself. My name is Stanley Madeley (by deed poll) and I am the UK's top Richard Madeley lookalike and a fifteen-year veteran entertainer of Britain's holiday camps. As a man who has adopted coats of many colours, I write to you, as a last measure, calling upon your very high reputation among red, green, and blue coats in order to help a fellow artist in need. Please permit me to explain ...

If you could picture the scene: I was working at a camp on the Dorset coast, providing quality children's entertainment with Fred and Ginger, my two trained stoats. It was about half past three in the afternoon and the children had become, as all children tend around that time, excitable and prone to mischief. I was just beginning a stunt I have done a thousand times before, placing Ginger down my oversized comedy trousers, when a young girl ran up and proceeded to strike me around my nethers with a hockeystick. A typical childish prank, I suppose, only this one managed to nail Ginger hard against my right buttock. Ginger, usually possessed of the most passive nature, became enraged, causing her to nip a part of me that's best not mentioned except to a family planning councillor. Unfortunately, as you'll know, once a stoat has a victim between its teeth, its jaws lock and it's impossible to disengage them without resorting to violence. Unfortunately, the pain was so great that I forgot about my audience and I resorted to violence. I won't go into graphic detail but the piano lid was off its hinges when I'd finished. There was one dead stoat and twenty-five distraught pre-teens in the room when the police and ambulances arrived.

But rest assured, Su, I have now written letters of apology to all of the children involved and I have also included photographs of Ginger II, in the hope that they'll believe the little biter was merely stunned by the piano lid (how could she have been?). However, my career is ruined. I have been stripped of my cabaret blazer and I doubt if I'll ever work on the South coast again.

Which brings me to my reason for writing: I have a new act that I'm promoting on the cabaret circuit. It too involves stoats though they won't be going down my trousers and will remain in clear view of the audience at all times. Because of my recent history, I'm looking to get some celebrity endorsements for my act. If by any chance in November you'd be in the area of Beckley (10th), Nuneaton (14th) or Chelmsford (18th), and you could come along and take part in my stage act, people might begin to trust me again. You would have to do very little. I'd simply put a stoat on your head where it would catch an arrow fired from a prop crossbow.

Failing a personal appearance, could you write me an endorsement saying you think 'Stan Madeley's stoat act is the best stoat act in the country!'

Thanking you for your time,

To: stan@stanmadeley.com
From: Jessica Williamson <████████████>
Date: 24/09/2009 16:25
Subject:

Dear Stan,

Thanks for your letter to Su. I'm afraid that due to her extremely busy schedule she won't be able to take part.

All the best with your show

Jessica

Noel Gay
19 Denmark Street
London
www.noelgay.com

Sandra, get this to the newspapers:

There once was a Pollard called Su,
Whose assistant's emails were rude.
No support she would lend,
To a man on the mend,
After his genitals were
   weasily chewed!

STAN MADELEY
THE UK'S TOP RICHARD MADELEY LOOKALIKE
BM NOUMENON, LONDON, WC1N 3XX   EMAIL: STAN@STANMADELEY.COM

Sir Freddie 'Black Rod' Viggers
Palace of Westminster
London, SW1A 0AA

18th November, 2009

Dear Freddie,

Just got in from the allotment and I've finally had chance to rewind the old Sky+ box to watch this morning's recording of the Queen's Speech. I had been expecting great things from you, sir, and I was not disappointed!

Allow me to introduce myself. The name is Stanley Madeley (by deed poll) and I'm the UK's top Richard Madeley lookalike, working in cabaret across the nation. You might have heard about my one-man show, 'Vulgar Bulgarian Zither – The Stanley Madeley Experience!' which often plays union bars in the Westminster village.

I am also something of a parliamentary buff and I like to rate the Black Rods as they come and go. I am writing because, quite frankly, you've raised the bar for future Gentlemen Ushers. I've not seen a debut performance like that since Admiral Sir Frank Twiss did his turn back in the 1970s. You strode towards the Commons with a real zeal, sir, and it fairly made the heart race. I would not have liked to have been the person who dared slam the door in your face.

Indeed, there was something quite magisterial about the way you hammered on that wood. Some Black Rods just never get it right. They never convey the right air of focussed indignation on behalf of the Lords. I'm thinking, of course, about dear old Sir John Gingell who didn't so much hammer on the door as politely tap. But there was no doubt that they'd answer your call.

As for your legs: A1. I have to say that they were certainly top class from this angle. Sir Michael Willcocks had good legs but he didn't have your knees. They were splendid things to see in stockings. It would not be too much of an exaggeration to say that my dear wife, Sandra (54), swooned when she saw them. I also felt a little light-headed.

Listen, I hope this isn't too much to ask but it's a tradition I've maintained for the past thirty-odd years. Do you think it's possible for a signed photo? I'd love one of you in your ceremonial gear, preferably showing off a little ankle. It will go in my album of Black Rods, with a little note to myself to the effect that I should watch this promising newcomer. You are already well on your way to eclipsing Hull, Stewart and Steiger and becoming my favourite Rod.

I remain, your humble fan,

Stan Madeley

Dear Stuart,

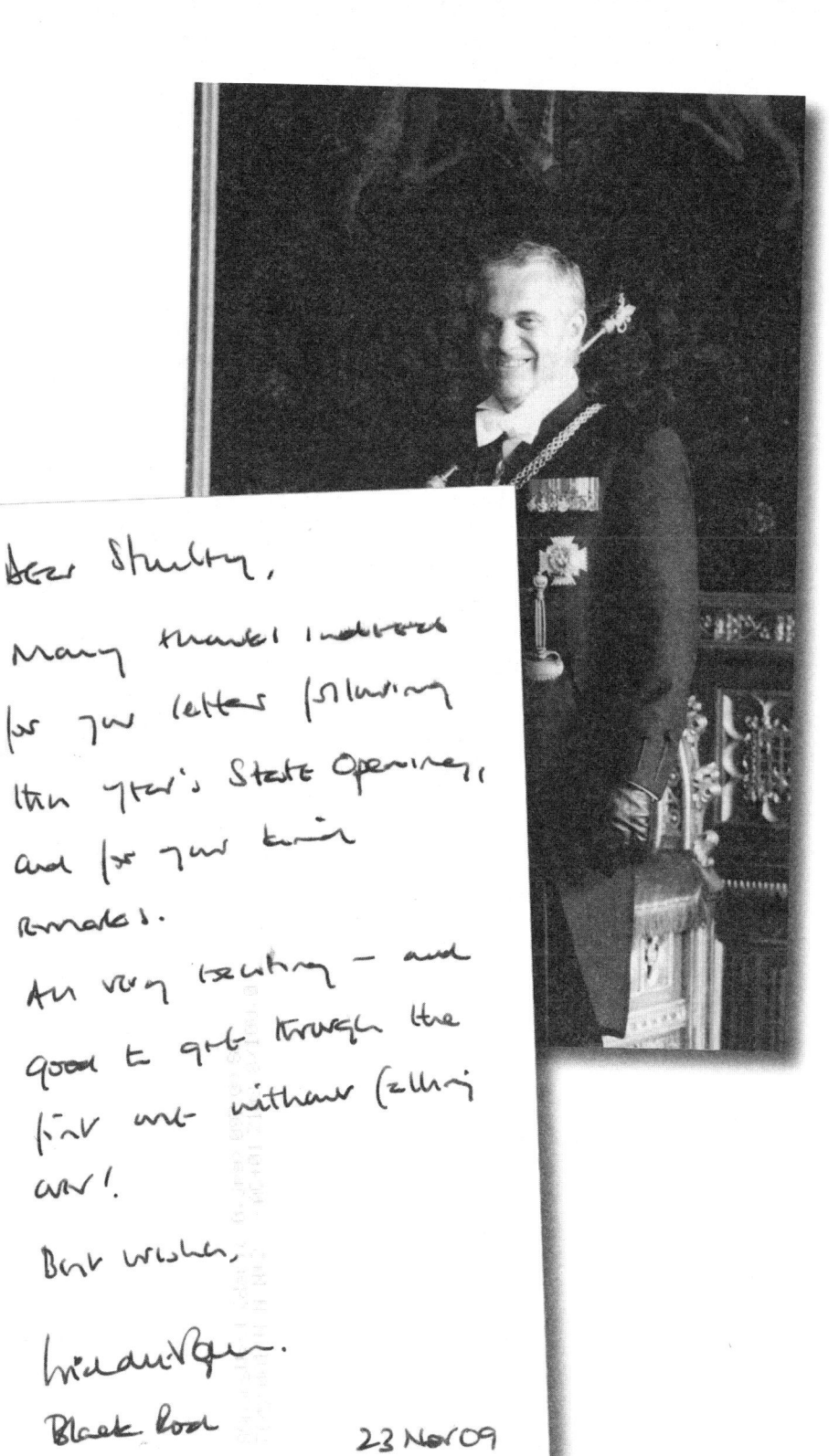

Many thanks indeed for your letter following this year's State Opening, and for your kind remarks.

All very exciting — and good to get through the first one without falling over!

Best wishes,

Michael Wilcox
Black Rod

23 Nov 09

STAN MADELEY
THE UK'S TOP RICHARD MADELEY LOOKALIKE
BM NOUMENON, LONDON, WC1N 3XX   EMAIL: STAN@STANMADELEY.COM

Dr. Rowan Williams
The Archbishop of Canterbury
Lambeth Palace, London

2nd January, 2010

Your Grace,

Finally managed to read a transcript of your words from Copenhagen and I'm totally behind you on this one. The environment is clearly the single most pressing issue to affect the world and it behoves us all to work to reduce our carbon footprints. That's why I decided to give up tissues this year.

But, please, allow me to introduce myself. The name is Stanley Madeley (by deed poll) and I'm a cabaret performer of some note as well as being the UK's top Richard Madeley lookalike. I don't expect you to have heard of me, but I do think you might have caught wind (pun intended) of my energy-saving schemes that have helped businesses turn green the length and breadth of Swindon.

I was struck by your words and, in particular, your belief that 'we are afraid because we don't know how we can survive without the comforts of our existing lifestyle'. That's bang on the money. Too many vested interests and an unwillingness to change: these are the problems facing us all. The only positive news is that there are open-minded chaps like you around. And that's why I thought I would write with my idea which I'm sure will help the church cut its energy costs dramatically.

Two words for you, Rowan ... Bell towers.

Think about it for just a minute. The Church of England possesses the biggest wind farm in the UK. It's just that nobody has ever thought about it in these terms. My plan would involve the installation of a suitably designed wind turbine atop the bell tower of every church in this country. I have included a rough design (seagull for scale and comic effect), though the final design of the blade would befit the architecture and the religious status of the towers. Just imagine half a dozen of these beauties perched atop Winchester Cathedral! Wouldn't that make those Nordic types jealous?

It also strikes me (another pun intended) that you have a large and able workforce of people willing to ring bells. But why should we allow so much of this renewable energy to go to waste? If we connected the ropes to an electric generator, the very act of ringing church bells would herald a new green economy. With a suitable clutch mechanism, we could disconnect the bells whenever we'd need a little peace and quiet, thus allowing the bell ringers to carry on practising and, in the process, producing free electricity twenty-four hours a day, straight into the national grid.

I'm sure that with a little reflection, you will see that it's not only viable but likely to attract huge numbers of converts to the faith.

Per Angusta Ad Augusta,

The Envirofix
a morally superior wind turbine

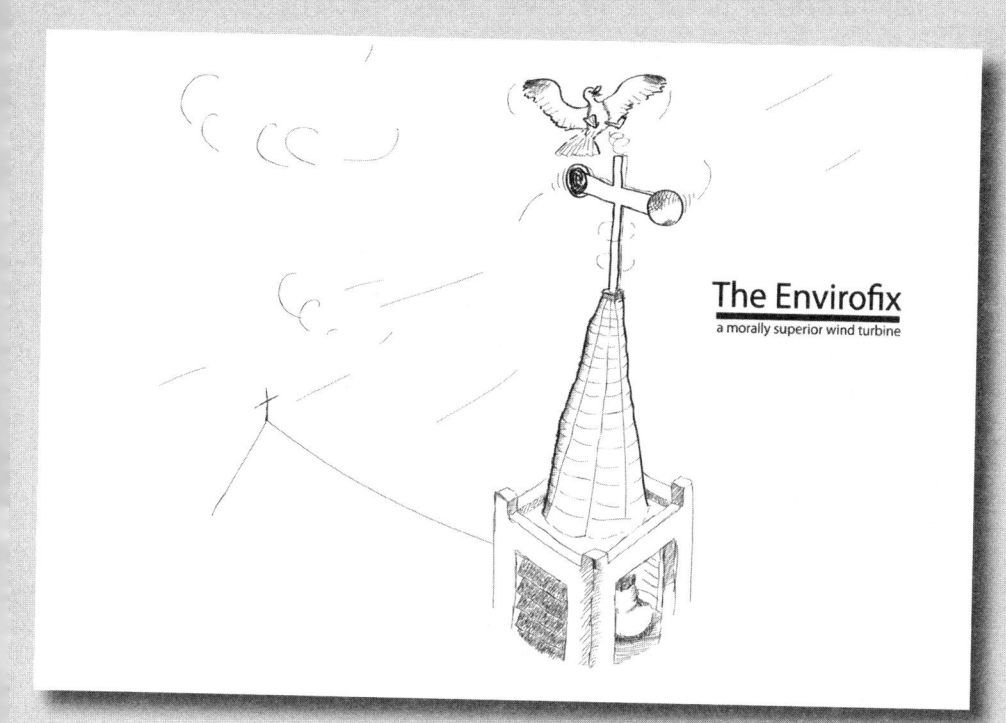

Dear Stan

The Archbishop thinks it's a sure prize winner and wishes you luck in negotiating with each of the 16,000 parish churches in England alone (to say nothing of the cathedrals of which, incidentally, I believe Salisbury has the highest spire).

Go for it.

Best wishes

Tim Livesey

STAN MADELEY
THE UK'S TOP RICHARD MADELEY LOOKALIKE
BM NOUMENON, LONDON, WC1N 3XX   EMAIL: STAN@STANMADELEY.COM

British Sausage Week   25th September, 2009
BPEX (AHDB)
Stoneleigh Park, Kenilworth
Warwickshire, CV8 2TL

Dear Sausage Lovers,

Allow me to introduce myself. My name is Stanley Madeley (by deed poll) and I am the UK's top Richard Madeley lookalike working in cabaret with my one-man show, 'Calibrated Midget Carnival – The Stanley Madeley Experience Live!'. I am also a working butcher with my own line of speciality bangers.

I am writing, in the first instance, to congratulate you for naming Paul Daniels and Debbie McGee as this year's faces of 'British Sausage Week'. Knowing both Paul and Debbie personally, I believe that you couldn't have chosen better! Both wife and self had spent many months anticipating the announcement yet, despite our contacts inside showbiz, it still took us by surprise. Sandra (54) was sure it was going to be Ringo Starr, whilst I had placed a crafty little bet on Princess Caroline of Monaco.

The main purpose of my writing, however, is to ask whether I'd need official sanction to hold my own sausage-themed events under the 'British Sausage Week' banner. Having established a strong brand name on the cabaret circuit, I am eager to make use of it by promoting my new line of heavily spiced sausages.

Just for your information: I will be wearing my sausage-meat suit the entire week. My act will involve sausages wherever possible. So, out go the balloon animals as I'll be twisting sausages into lots of clever and cunning shapes. I will also be performing some sausage bending, sausage swallowing, sausage magic, as well as singing some sausage-themed songs, including my medley of Simon and Garfunkel hits, 'The Sound of Sausage', 'Bridge Over Troubled Sausage', and, of course, 'Hazy Shade of Sausage'. It sounds like crazy fun and I'm sure it will be! Yet, for me, the highlight of the celebrations will undoubtedly be my wife's world record attempt to weave the largest wicker basket made entirely from strings of sausages. Sandra (54) has been practising for months and it's sure to be a fantastic achievement if she can get up to the fourteen-foot mark.

All told, I think we've got an excellent programme of entertainment planned and I would very much hope that you agree. I'm sure that 'Uncle Stan's Bangers' will be a hit with customers who prefer more exotic meats in their diet and I hope to see you all when the festivities commence on Monday 2nd November.

Very best wishes!

BPEX
Marketing

Mr S Madeley
BM Noumenon
London
WC1N 3XX

29 September 2009

Dear Stan

Thank you for your letter dated 25 September 2009. It certainly sounds like you have exciting plans for British Sausage Week!

As the name suggests the prime purpose of the week is to promote British Pork Sausages on behalf of pig farmers in Britain. Consequently, if your act and range of sausages serve the same purpose I would be happy for you to hold events under the British Sausage Week banner.

If you could kindly send us details of your events and sausage range, we may be able to promote them on our website.

Yours sincerely

Tina Mulholland
Product Manager

BPEX BPEX is a division of the Agriculture and Horticulture Development Board

STAN MADELEY
THE UK'S TOP RICHARD MADELEY LOOKALIKE
BM NOUMENON, LONDON, WC1N 3XX   EMAIL: STAN@STANMADELEY.COM

Mr. John Prescott   3rd November, 2009

Dear John,

Forgive the intrusion, as I have been forced to forgive your very regrettable retirement from public life. And, please, allow me to introduce myself. The name is Stanley Madeley (by deed poll) and I'm the UK's top Richard Madeley lookalike, currently working in cabaret with my hoop-jumping Alsatians, Tony & Gordon.

I write with two purposes. The first is to encourage you to return to front-line politics. Westminster life has become so dull since you took a step back that Charles Clarke is now considered a 'personality'. I'm sorry, John, but the nation demands you to take a step forward, perhaps even two. I am sure, if you were to make yourself available, the party would back you for the very top job.

My second purpose for writing is to congratulate you for your recent documentary detailing the differences between the north and south. As a born and bred northerner (even, dare I say, more northern than you, given that you were born in Wales), I was motivated to write to say that you've changed my opinion of the south.

Listening to that craven fool, Sewell, jabbering on about northerners lacking the intellect to make the leap from the spoken to written word, it disgusted me to the bottom of my ... you know ... my ... well ... to the soles of my loafers. I always thought that southerners looked on me kindly, almost as one of their own. Only now, I find myself plagued by a new-found paranoia. John, I swear that they are all mocking me behind my back! Whenever I go out on stage, I'm aware that my accent sounds strange and alien, my vowels too flat. That laughter from the crowd: it's not laughter. It's scorn! And it's ruining me as a performer and as a man.

Since watching your documentary, I can't look a southern crowd in the eye without wanting to tell them what I think about their soft southern lifestyles, their middle-class ambitions, their banal musings about the novels of George Eliot. They can stick their cucumber sandwiches in their aristocratically sizeable earholes. I eat chip butties, John, and I'm proud that I do.

Then there are the cravats, ginger-haired men called Simon, chutney, Vinnie Jones, Henley on Thames, Michael Gove, squirrels, Nicholas Parsons ... They might mock us for our pork scratchings but do you know what it is? It's pork scratching envy. Yet they eat jellied eels! Even their pigeons are feral. Southerners are just a bunch of mollusc-scoffing, aristocratically inbred, Cockney, dung-shovelling, Hansom cab-riding, gaiter-wearing members of the ruling elite, all related to the same jug-eared Duke of Fitzwhatever.

Anyway, wife and self have now decided to move back north. We're looking to buy property in Hull, so if you know of any, I'd be grateful.

Keep the red flag flying!

HOUSE OF COMMONS
LONDON SW1A 0AA

The Office of
The Rt Hon John Prescott MP

30 November 2009

Dear Stanley

Thank you for your very amusing letter. I am looking forward to retirement at the next election, but thanks for trying to yank me out of it!

With best wishes

JohnPrescott

Rt Hon John Prescott MP

Stanley Madeley
BM Noumenon
London
WC1N 3XX

STAN MADELEY
THE UK'S TOP RICHARD MADELEY LOOKALIKE
BM NOUMENON, LONDON, WC1N 3XX   EMAIL: STAN@STANMADELEY.COM

Mr. Brian Sewell
c/o London Evening Standard
2 Derry Street
London, W8 5TT

19th October, 2009

Dear Mr. Sewell,

Allow me to introduce myself. My name is Stanley Madeley (by deed poll) and I am the UK's top Richard Madeley lookalike, currently 'packing them in' with my one-man Dadaist cabaret, 'Valette's Donkeyskin Purse – The Stanley Madeley Experience Live!' at the Salford Empire.

Sir, I stand in awe of your command of words and the clarity of your judgements. I speak, of course, about the contribution you made last week on the TV show featuring the nation's favourite northern lout, Mr. John Prescott. I applauded the remarks you made in 2005, wishing that those in the north-west would succumb to the pox or the Russian flu, and I'm even more supportive of the views you expressed in this programme. My wife, Sandra (54), has wanted the north annexed for a long time but the notion of wiping out northerners with a good dose of flu excited her even more.

As you might note from the postmark, I am writing this from the enemy heartland. I am often stuck up here due to tour commitments and it leaves me suffering an ennui like no other. Northerners eat poorly, dress poorly, speak poorly, and have a generally poor attitude towards everything, especially mental work. You asked how northerners make the intellectual leap from the spoken to the written word: simply, sir, they do not! They speak in syllables, grunts, or flaccid snorts. The closest these people come to art is to wallow in kitsch, which holds pride of place in the centre of every mill town. I was travelling through St. Helens recently and witnessed the monstrosity of Jaume Plensa's 'Dream'. Dream! It's more like a bloody nightmare! Yet it somehow fits this wasteland of grey flannelette sweat-suits and surly men with shaved eyebrows. This is not regeneration. It's reanimation; another horrendous attempt by central government to waste southern taxes on the festering cadaver of a grim post-war northern industrial landscape. A plague would be a kindness, though I doubt if people north of Watford could even spell the word.

One is reminded of Jonathan Swift's suggestion that the Irish poor should eat their babies, but to offer a similar observation here would be to advocate an unhealthy diet. Never have I seen such fat children! To eat a baby would send a man's cholesterol soaring. These people are repulsive enough that they might just try it. Thank you, again, for expressing what so many of us have thought but dare not utter. I enclose an envelope in the hope that you might send a supportive word or two, possibly scribbled on the back of a signed photo of your extremely handsome self.

I remain, your most humble servant,

Stanley Madeley (Southerner)

From: BRIAN SEWELL 25. xi 09.

Evening Standard
2 Derry Street, London W8 5EE
Tel: 020 7938 6000

Thanks for your letter. Alas, I know nothing of the other Richard Madeley – that point thus eludes me – but we seem to be in broad agreement over other matters. As for eating habits, my proposal for a recipe book on the matter based on a manuscript fragment believed to be by HARPAGUS, has been rejected by Thames and Hudson, though they quite liked [illegible] drawings for it.

With best wishes –

Brian Sewell –

English translation:

Thanks for your letter. Alas, I know nothing of the other Richard Madeley – that point thus eludes me – but we seem to be in broad agreement over other matters. As for eating habits, my proposal for a recipe book on the matter based on a manuscript fragment believed to be by HARPAGUS has been rejected by Thames and Hudson, though they quite liked [illegible] drawings for it.

With best wishes –
Brian Sewell

STAN MADELEY
THE UK'S TOP RICHARD MADELEY LOOKALIKE
BM NOUMENON, LONDON, WC1N 3XX   EMAIL: STAN@STANMADELEY.COM

David 'Conk' Vaughan
The Membership Secretary
Clowns International,
~~[redacted]~~
~~[redacted]~~

10th November, 2009

Honk! Honk! My dear Conk!

Sniff my flower and call me Nuts! And, please, allow me to introduce myself! The name is Stanley Madeley (by deed poll) though my friends do indeed call me Nuts the Clown. Not only am I the UK's top Richard Madeley lookalike but I'm also a circus performer of some 15 years in the business of throwing paper-filled buckets.

Forgive the lateness of the introduction but I've only just been informed of your existence by my friend Mr. Bongo and his good wife Mrs. Bobo. Naturally, now that I know of your excellent association, I am eager to join. However, I have a few reservations and I hope that you can satisfy my questions before I whip out my oversized purse and send you some coins.

First of all, I am seeking your assurance that Bill 'Ploppy' Bunall isn't part of Clowns International. In the past we have come to blows, Ploppy and I, and you might even go to say that he's my sworn enemy. I swear, he once tried to mow me down whilst driving his clown car on Skegness seafront. It was meant to be a fun afternoon of carnival entertainment for the children but it ended with the pair of us handcuffed to radiators in the local police station.

Secondly, what kind of incentives do you offer for practising clowns? I gather there is a 'World Clown Association' that offers discounts on merchandise. My big shoes are wearing thin but I'm loath to replace them given the cost. If you could get me 10% off my next pair, I would certainly take up your membership offer.

My final enquiry is of a sensitive nature, which I hope you can treat with the utmost discretion. Indeed, Conk, it goes to the very heart of why I've chosen to write to you now. Do you offer any kind of legal service for those of us whose clowning has occasionally strayed into illegality? I tell you why I ask. I was recently performing my chisel-throwing routine (highly commended, by the way) when the chisel slipped from my white-gloved hand and grazed a youngster sitting in the audience about a dozen feet away. Thankfully it left only a gash and missed her eye by a good centimetre and a half. However, at the time, I was worried that without an official body of clowns to defend me, I might lose everything, even the sleeveless shirt from my back. My current legal council is doing a poor job defending me over a separate incident involving a pair of oversized trousers which fell down due to substandard pink braces. The Women's Institute has started legal proceedings but the incident has yet to go to court.

I thank you for your attention and eagerly await your fun water-based response.

Keep spraying the children!

[signature]

Stanley 'Nuts' Madeley

CLOWNS INTERNATIONAL
From The Secretary

Visit Clowns International at www.clowns-international.com

24 November 2009

Mr S Madeley
BM Noumenon
London
WC1N 3XX

Dear Mr Madeley

Thank you for your letter of 10th November addressed to the Membership Secretary of this club. With regard to information about Clowns International, its aims and objects etc., may I refer you to our website, the address of which can be found at the head of this letter. A membership application form can be downloaded from this site.

With regard to your comments about legal representation and discounts etc., I would presume that you are a member of Equity so that organisation can provide you with what you are seeking in this respect.

The names of the persons you quote in your letter are not known to Clowns International.

Clowns International is essentially a social club for Clown Artistes and is the oldest organisation of its kind in the world. Its members are required to hold Criminal Records Bureau Clearance certificates and Public Liability Insurance cover when performing.

I trust that this information will be helpful to you.

Yours sincerely

Tony Eldridge
Secretary
Clowns International

Hon President	Chairman	Secretary	Treasurer
Ron Moody	Gordon Sharpe	Tony Eldridge	Chris Fincham

STAN MADELEY
THE UK'S TOP RICHARD MADELEY LOOKALIKE
BM NOUMENON, LONDON, WC1N 3XX   EMAIL: STAN@STANMADELEY.COM

Tom O'Connor c/o
Positive Management
PO Box 161, Ormskirk

15th September, 2009

Dear Tom,

Allow me to introduce myself. My name is Stanley Madeley (by deed poll) and I am the UK's top Richard Madeley lookalike. If you've not heard of me as 'The Spoon Magician', perhaps you know me as Dr. Spring from TV's *Unit: ENT*.

As you might know, a TV producer recently saw my act at the Edinburgh Fringe and has asked me to film a pilot for *That's My Noodle*, a cookery quiz show based on the popular Norwegian hit *Sbrark Ma Nurgleshk*. The rules are simple. Blindfolded, a contestant is fed a variety of strange, exotic and occasionally diabolical dishes. Some have been prepared by the best chefs in the country, whilst the others have been slapped together by imbecilic members of the general public or Heston Blumenthal. If the contestant can guess who has made the dish based on the blindfolded taste test, they win the prize. The producers have asked me to study the original series to borrow a few of the techniques of the popular Norwegian host, Torolav Schønemann. However, I've decided to do it my own way. I have spent the past month watching *Play That Tune*, *Gambit* and *Cross Wits* for 16 hours a day. I now think I've got your technique off pat and I wanted to know if you think I'm onto a winner.

1. Show begins. I'm in a white suit, white shirt, bright blue dickey and carrying an oddly shaped microphone like a lozenge attached to a ladle (it's the cookery theme, you see, Tom). I run down from the audience, stopping to kiss one or two or to shake their hand should they possess a moustache.

2. I speak: 'Hello and welcome to another episode of *That's My Noodle*, the brand new culinary TV quiz show with me, Stan Madeley.'

3. I then hit them with a few jokes. 'You know, I love food. I really do. And the more exotic the better. I won't eat anything unless David Attenborough has allowed it to sit on his head. But I'm not saying that I'm not environmental ... Well, okay, I *am* saying I'm not environmental but I will not eat any endangered species. I mean they're so hard to find ... Seriously, though, I believe that the best way to save animals is to turn them into profitable luxury goods. The day Tesco start selling Sperm Burgers is the day that I know that we've managed to save the whale.'

4. I then introduce the contestants, ask them to recount some funny anecdote involving public indecency or accidents with pets, before we launch into the first round and I cash my pay cheque.

So, Tom, what's your professional opinion? Am I onto a winner? If you don't think I have the knack, I'll tell them to forget the show and I'll go back to the cabaret circuit where I at least shared rooms with strippers.

Kind regards,

Stan Madeley

PS. Any chance of a signed photo for my mother? She thinks of you as a silver-haired Richard Gere but without the Buddhism. Her name is Barbara.

Love to Barbara
Tom O'Connor

Great idea Stan but it needs to build to a climax. Could be a winner if you get away with references to animals being turned into luxury goods!!

Good luck

Tom.

With Compliments

Tom O'Connor

ASCOT

STAN MADELEY
THE UK'S TOP RICHARD MADELEY LOOKALIKE
BM NOUMENON, LONDON, WC1N 3XX EMAIL: STAN@STANMADELEY.COM

Steve Jebson
Commercial Director, Superdrug
118 Beddington Lane
Croydon, Surrey CR0 4TB

15th February, 2010

Dear Steve,

I am writing about the difference that a 'd' makes.

You see, due to poor reviews which you might have seen reprinted in the national press recently, I am about to retire from my work as a professional lookalike (the UK's top Richard Madeley double, to be precise). I intend to devote my energies to a small shop I plan to open with my wife Sandra (54) who has herself been involved in the hair and make-up business at the top level for twenty-seven years. She has worked with some of the UK's top stars (Su Pollard), ensuring they look good, so she clearly knows what she's doing.

The gap in the retail market we intend to exploit is that of the hand-made luxury hair piece, and we wondered if your company would have any problem with our calling the shop 'Superrug'.

By dropping the 'd', we think we're making it quite clear that we'd have no connection with your excellent enterprise. Rather, because we're in the toupee-making business, we think we will complement your business quite well, though catering to a different customer base. We expect Superrug's punters to be older, more affluent, and generally of a much classier demographic. To be blunt: experience has taught us that very few seventeen-year-old dental hygienists called Chantelle require a hairpiece!

Levity aside, I suppose you want to know more about us. Well, our toupees are made from hair imported from only the best villages in South-East Asia, though we will have a luxury line made from hair sourced in Scandinavian countries. We will also be providing the very best advice and counselling for toupee wearers. My wife thinks it important to change people's perceptions of hairpieces, countering so much bad publicity that toupees have received over the last decade (Bruce Forsyth) and to encourage best practice among both wig makers and wig wearers.

We will naturally wait for you to give us the all-clear before we pay for any signage outside our shop, located near Southwold's fish market.

Let me finish by saying that both wife and self are very frequent shoppers at Superdrug and hold your business model up as an example that clearly works.

I remain, your friend in cabaret,

Stan Madeley

42

Superdrug

Superdrug Stores plc
A member of the A.S. Watson Group

118 Beddington Lane
Croydon
Surrey CR0 4TB
United Kingdom
Tel +44 (0)20 8684 7000
Fax +44 (0)20 8684 6102

Stan Madeley
BM Noumenon
London
WC1N 3XX

15 March 2010

Dear Mr Madeley

Thank you for your letter dated 15 February addressed to our Commercial Director, Steve Jebson.

You have explained that you wish to call your new shop "Superrug", and have requested our approval to use this name. Unfortunately we cannot agree to your use of the name "Superrug", as we consider it sounds too similar to Superdrug. We operate over 900 stores throughout the UK and Ireland. We have built up significant goodwill in the Superdrug brand over the last 40 years and would not want any confusion between Superdrug and your business. Furthermore we sell hair pieces and accessories in our stores and therefore there is some overlap with your proposed product.

We trust that you will find a suitable alternative name for your shop. Please be advised that we take the protection of our brand extremely seriously and will take action if we feel it is being compromised.

Yours sincerely

**Sally Chandler
Legal Manager**

Health and beauty stores of
Hutchison Whampoa Limited
Registered office: 118 Beddington Lane, Croydon, Surrey, CR0 4TB. Registered in England & Wales. Company No. 807043

Health & Beauty from A.S. Watson

STAN MADELEY
THE UK'S TOP RICHARD MADELEY LOOKALIKE
BM NOUMENON, LONDON, WC1N 3XX   EMAIL: STAN@STANMADELEY.COM

Derren Brown c/o
Michael Vine Associates
1 Stormont Road, London

5th October, 2009

Dear Derren,

Allow me to introduce myself. My name is Stanley Madeley (by deed poll) and I am the foremost Richard Madeley lookalike currently working in the country. **YOU** are possibly wondering why I'm writing. After all, you probably didn't catch my sell-out surrealist show, 'Pink Nun Chew – The Stanley Madeley Experience Live' at this year's Edinburgh Fringe. However, I'm quietly confident that you would have enjoyed it if you had. It **WILL** come as no surprise that I too am an aficionado of conjuration, having worked fifteen years as a stage illusionist, specialising in tricks involving rabbits, doves, parrots and lizards (I have large hands). Indeed, just when I'm about to go on stage, my charming wife, Sandra (you would like her), will often **SEND** me text messages full of sound advice regarding our profession. 'Never blame your weasel when your tricks go wrong!' is one I live by.

But enough chit chat. Let me get down to my reason for writing. It fills **ME** with great sadness to inform you, Mr. Brown, that our good friend and mentor to magicians everywhere, Ernest P. Wittlepool, died last week at the age of 103. This grand old gentleman was one of the pioneering magicians of his day, though his name is rarely known outside of magic circles (pun intended). As you will know, he invented the Wittlepool Knot, the most innovative magical knot, which has helped countless generations of magicians keep their trousers up. He will be missed greatly by those of us at 'The Association of Conjurers & Mind Benders', where he served as President for 24 years. However, life must go on and at last night's meeting of the Association, we drew **LOTS** and your name came out top, three votes ahead of that of Debbie McGee. Therefore, it falls to me, as the Association's treasurer, to inform you that we have named you our new Honorary Chairman and we have awarded you the title **OF** 'High Mage of Elemental Conjuration & Mind Benderyness'. I'm sorry to say that the title means little to the wider magician community but there are no real duties of which to speak. Indeed, the position comes with no **MONEY** or financial incentive. However, we're quite sure you're used to that, what with you having worked for Channel 4 for so long.

I would be very grateful if you could acknowledge whether you'll be accepting the title **AND** if you'd be available for the fitting of robes in the near future. I don't know if you're familiar with the High Wickham town centre but there's a very good shop, next door to the hairdresser's, that sells all manner of costumes. My wife often shops there and can't say enough good things about their extensive range of magician's capes, **MONKEY** suits and ball gowns. Anyway, it was a pleasure writing to you. Switching **HATS** for a moment, might I conclude this letter as a fan, saying how much I've enjoyed your work over a number of years. You might even say that I hope that your tricks might yet make me a very rich man!

I remain, your most humble servant,

[signature]

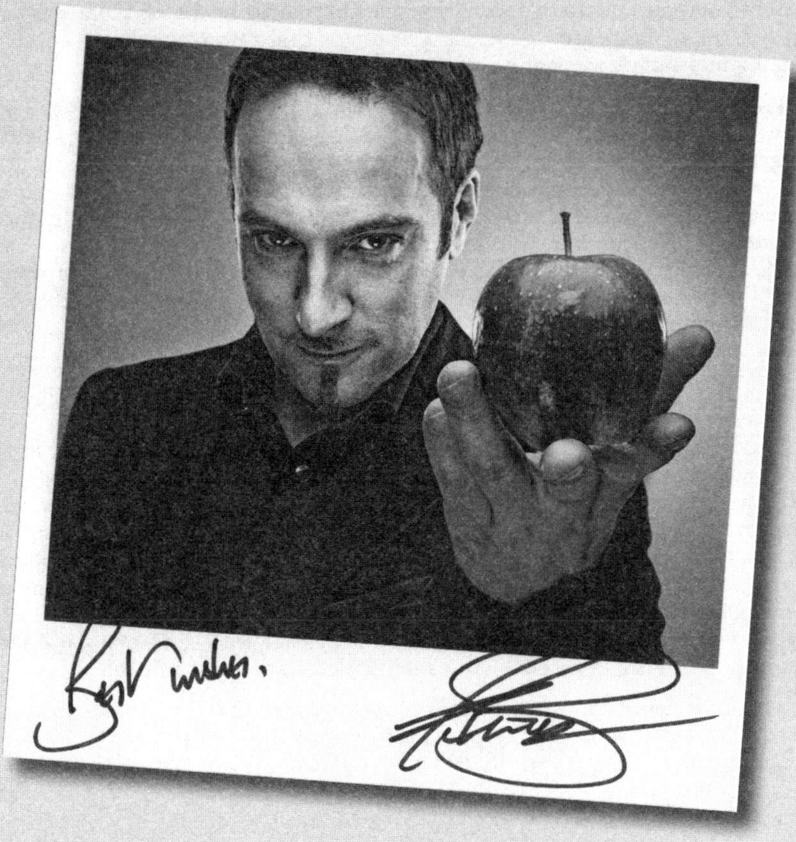
Best wishes.

STAN MADELEY
THE UK'S TOP RICHARD MADELEY LOOKALIKE
BM NOUMENON, LONDON, WC1N 3XX   EMAIL: STAN@STANMADELEY.COM

Derren Brown c/o
Michael Vine Associates
1 Stormont Road, London

2nd November, 2009

Dear Derren,

Delighted, sir! Absolutely delighted to have received your reply and, what's more, to have done so in the middle of a postal strike. It was a miracle! One of your best tricks yet! I'm not sure what you meant to convey by sending me a picture of you holding an apple but there's clearly something clever in that too. Since it arrived last week, I've had a craving for Cox's pippins that I can't otherwise explain. In fact, it's more than a craving. I can't get enough of my Cox's!

And here's the thing ... Last Friday morning, less than a week after your picture arrived, I withdrew all the savings from wife and self's bank account and bought an apple orchard in Surrey. I don't know a thing about running an apple orchard and I know even less about Surrey. Thankfully, I'm married to a good woman or she might have blanched when I withdrew £240,000 and gambled it on apples. Sandra (54) believes that you have something planned. So certain is she that you're about to burst through the front door that she can't sit down to watch the TV without drawing the curtains back so your camera crew can get a good view of the new flock wallpaper.

I suppose this will be one of your A1 specials for Channel 4? 'Derren Brown's Apple A Day ...' Jolly good wheeze, though I hope I'm not going to be stuck with this ruddy apple orchard. I've already had to sack the head apple keeper who refused to listen to my suggestion to improve the yield of the trees. His family might have been in the business for nearly two hundred years but mine have been professional mimes, blackguards, traitors, convicts, sailors, harpsichordists, ointment salesmen, rigidity inspectors and odd jobbers for twice that long. But you can't get the staff these days. People just mechanically go about their work, opening envelopes, stuffing and shuffling forms, posting things off ... They don't appreciate when somebody goes to the great trouble of crafting a letter, full of wit and wonder. Sometimes, Derren, it's like dealing with unthinking drones, brainwashed by some fiendish genius with a skill for mind control!

So, whatever you have planned, Derren, you can count me in. To tell you the truth, what I needed in my life was a picture of you holding fruit. I just can't get that picture out of my mind. It's like you have me in a hypnotic spell. It's as though I'm aware of the world around me, yet I'm not in full control of my senses ... I suppose it's a bit like watching BBC2.

Anyway, I'm sure you know what you're doing with my brain so feel free to play with it without my knowledge whenever you like. I have faith in you, D.B.! Sandra asks if you could send her a signed photo of you pointing at a runner bean. Women! You give them fruit and they want vegetables!

Keep plugging away,

Stan Madeley

> Sandra, your eyes grow heavy and you have an urge to make me a cup of tea... perhaps with a couple of chocolate HobNobs...

STAN MADELEY
THE UK'S TOP RICHARD MADELEY LOOKALIKE
BM NOUMENON, LONDON, WC1N 3XX EMAIL: STAN@STANMADELEY.COM

Michelle Mone
Ultimo Bras
MJM International Ltd
8 Redwood Crescent
Glasgow, G74 5PA

22nd September, 2009

Re. Brassieres

Dear Ms. Mone,

Allow me to introduce myself. My name is Stanley Madeley (by deed poll) and, as you might intuit from my business stationery, I am the UK's leading Richard Madeley lookalike. I am writing to you, however, on a matter of great sensitivity. You see, as a man of a certain age and of a certain sedentary lifestyle, I have come to the point where I believe that I would be best served, hygienically speaking, by wearing a brassiere. Please don't laugh. My 'mounds' (I find the word 'moobs' offensive) are now at the stage where they are affecting my quality of life, as well as attracting comments from passing members of the public. Sometimes unwelcome comments.

Yet, nothing has been done about a condition that faces millions of men each year. Well, no more, I say! I have experienced a similar epiphany to yours, Michelle. After all, why must we men with minor glandular problems be forced to wear ugly vests that provide neither lift nor support? And a vest only encourages sweat to gather beneath our appendages, with the resulting problems of chafing, fungal infections, and/or mildew. Yet, all it would take is a single manufacturer with vision to address this issue. Then we might begin to see some progress!

To that end, might I suggest a range of male-only brassieres which have been designed with the large-breasted man in mind? Forget lacy frills and the colour pink: if you could produce them in black or camouflage, we'd be halfway to capturing the sizeable UK market for male mound support.

I have included my own design for my first brassiere with this letter. As you will see, it is modelled on the F-117 Nighthawk stealth bomber and would appeal to any man with breast problems and a love of military aviation. Perhaps we could sell them as the 'stealth-brassiere', undetectable by enemy radar? I can see the TV ads now: a man flies low over enemy terrain, protected by his stealth brassiere and the knowledge that his pendulous man-breasts are securely protected behind his 'bomb bay doors'. Can you see it now, Michelle? Can you see the millions we could make with this idea?

I'll leave you with that tantalising thought and, dare I say, appealing image.

Kind regards,

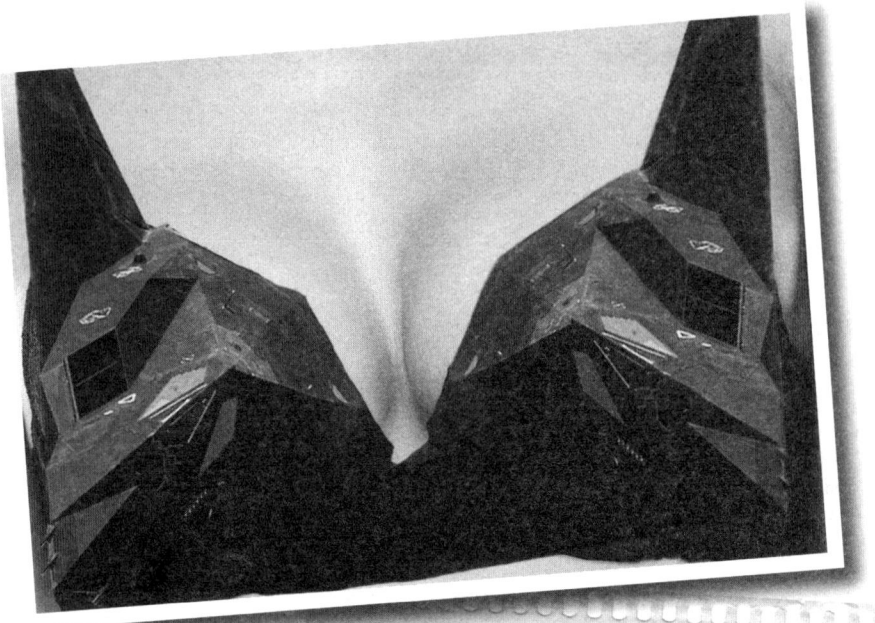

Sandra, if by some unlikely chance they don't like the bra idea, remind me to send them my design for a hat with knitted sleeves.

The Sou'Esther

mJm
INTERNATIONAL

11th November 2009

Mr Stanley Madeley
BM Noumenon
London
WC1N 3XX

Dear Mr Madeley

Many thanks for your recent letter.

Unfortunately at this moment in time we are fully committed solely to our brands and unable to look at further projects.

Thank you once again for contacting MJM International and we would like to wish you all the very best.

Yours sincerely

Laura Mair

Laura Mair
PA to Michelle Mone

MJM INTERNATIONAL LIMITED, 8 REDWOOD CRESCENT, PEEL PARK, EAST KILBRIDE G74 5PA
TEL: +44 (0) 845 812 0202   FAX: +44 (0) 845 812 0303   UK & Europe Retail Order Line: +44 (0) 845 230 1122
email: enquiries@mjm-international.com   www.mjm-international.com
REGISTERED IN SCOTLAND NO. 169601

STAN MADELEY
THE UK'S TOP RICHARD MADELEY LOOKALIKE
BM NOUMENON, LONDON, WC1N 3XX   EMAIL: STAN@STANMADELEY.COM

Lord Jeffrey Archer   9th March, 2010

Dear Lord Archer,

Now, look here. I'm no writer. My business is cabaret, though, believe it or not, I actually earn more as the UK's top Richard Madeley lookalike (two fifty a week and occasional wardrobe). I have never attempted to bang out a book, whereas you have a gift for words that I could only dream of possessing. That's why I have read and admired your blog since the day it first appeared on my laptop and why I finally feel compelled to write.

Not to complain, I hasten to add, but to save you. From whom, you ask? Why, from Your Lordship yourself! You see, I do know how to spot the fatal flaw in a hero and I believe I've spotted yours.

In your latest blog entry (2nd March, 2010), you write about attending a recent performance of *Measure for Measure*:

'Michael Attenborough's production fizzed from beginning to end, even if the plot creaks a little, with titters of laughter from a young audience.'

Now, let me get this straight: are you saying that William Shakespeare, supposedly the world's greatest dramatist, wrote a plot that 'creaks a little'? I'm sorry, Your Lordship. I might be one of your most devoted fans (admittedly, not the brightest) but I'm not sure that I follow you on this. Are you saying that you could do a better job?

Don't get me wrong: I've loved every one of your books and there wasn't a hole in the plot of any one of them that I could see. But, then again, I'm no critic. On the other hand, my wife, Sandra (54), is something of a literary bod and only reads the heavy-going stuff: Nabokov, Conrad, a little poetry by that bloke with the opium pipe going on about Zanussi. Even Sandra doesn't think that this play has plot problems. In fact, she was explaining (rather laboriously, to be honest) that the plot reflects the moral something or other of the inner drama. I could get her to write it out for you if you like.

I'm not writing to say you're wrong, Your Lordship, but I worry that you might be opening yourself up to a little mockery from the press if they get wind of this. I hope you don't mind but I've written to the UK's top authority on Shakespearean matters to see what he has to say. Should the press come calling, I suggest delaying tactics until we can get some authoritative statement.

Please give my best wishes to Her Ladyship, though I feel that she should really have a look over your shoulder before you post anything to your blog. I will end by saying that I am very much looking forward to your next book. If you ever want somebody to proofread it for you, I'd be only too glad to help.

Your friend in cabaret,

JEFFREY ARCHER

Mr S Madeley
B M Noumenon
London WC1N 3XX

17th March 2010

Dear Mr Madeley,
Many thanks for your letter of 9th March.

I wouldn't dream of comparing my work with Shakespeare, but critics and academics have pointed out in the past that *Measure for Measure* is not among the Bard's greatest works.

Thank you for reading the blog. My new book, *And Thereby Hangs a Tale,* will be published on May 21st. I do hope you enjoy it.

With best wishes

Yours sincerely

Jeffrey Archer

STAN MADELEY
THE UK'S TOP RICHARD MADELEY LOOKALIKE
BM NOUMENON, LONDON, WC1N 3XX EMAIL: STAN@STANMADELEY.COM

Abigail Francis
Membership Secretary
Association & Register of Colon Hydrotherapists
███████████████
███████████████

21st September, 2009

Dear Ms. Francis,

Excuse the intrusion (pun intended!). I'm just taking a wild punt here, in the hope that my practical experience will qualify me for membership to your excellent organisation. But first, please allow me to introduce myself. My name is Stanley Madeley (by deed poll) and I'm the UK's top Richard Madeley lookalike currently working the North London Cabaret circuit with my one-man surrealist show, 'Thumb Putty Theatre – The Stanley Madeley Experience Live!'.

I know you're probably wondering why such a successful and (dare I say?) handsome man in his late 50s should be writing to you, but, you see, it has always been my dream to be a colonic hydrotherapist. I do love to make people feel happy and I've always enjoyed handling hosepipe. And if that's not what it takes to take up a career in the colonic irrigation business then I don't know what is!

Since I've decided to develop my interest into a career, I have completed a home correspondence course via the Internet with one of America's most respected centres for colonic hydrotherapy. I now have a certificate in Anal Hygiene (photocopy enclosed) and I have been spending my weekends practising my technique, with my dear wife, Sandra (54), providing the willing body. I've now got the four stages of lubrication, application & insertion, nozzle jockeying and removal, down to art, with Sandra no longer complaining about any discomfort. In fact, she has been recommending me to her friends, many of whom have now undergone successful cleansings in our back bedroom.

Naturally, my correspondence course has made me acutely aware of the need to keep the place sanitised, so whilst we do run a long length of B&Q garden hose from the bathroom, along the landing, and into the back bedroom, we only empty buckets in the *downstairs* sink. However, if there's more than the usual amount of solids, we'll open a grid.

I hope my experience and enthusiasm will make up for my age and my lack of more formal qualifications. Please find my completed application form attached and I very much look forward to your reply. I cannot express how much this means to me and I have big plans should you allow me to join your organisation. My wife and I have already discussed having the back bedroom properly plumbed. But that, needless to say, awaits your decision. You hold my future in your (hopefully) warm fingers.

Happy flushings!

Stan Madeley

STAR SPANGLED COLLEGE OF THE COLON

THIS CERTIFICATE IS AWARDED TO:

STANLEY MADELEY

ON COMPLETING 'ANAL HYGIENE FOR BEGINNERS' WITH A DISTINCTION.

AWARDED BY
THE STAR SPANGLED COLON COLLEGE, UTAH,
ON THE AUGUST 23RD, 2009.

NOSTRUM
ANUS
TERSUS
UTPOTE
1973

ON BEHALF OF THE COLLEGE

ARCH

Membership Application Form

Please complete this form, **IN BLOCK CAPITALS PLEASE** and return it to the address below for processing.

Section 1 – Personal details	
Legal Surname	MADELEY (BY DEED POLL)
Professional Name *if different from above*	'THE SPOON MAGICIAN', 'THE AMAZING STAN', 'UNCLE SMUDGE', OR DR. SPRING FROM TV'S 'UNIT: ENT'.
First Names	STANLEY
Title	MR.
Gender	CABARET
Date of Birth	4/11/1954
Marital Status	HAPPILY MARRIED TO MY DEAR WIFE, SANDRA.
Nationality	ENGLISH BUT MY WIFE IS TECHNICALLY NORWEGIAN.
Home Address	BM NOUMENON LONDON
Post/area Code	WC1N 3XX
Home tel.	EX-DIRECTORY
Mobile tel.	FRIENDS, FAMILY AND OUTGOING EMERGENCY CALLS ONLY
email address	STAN@STANMADELEY.COM
Is English your first language? *If not, please state level of competency*	YES, I'D CONSIDER MYSELF SEMI-FLUENT

SECTION 2 – Professional details	
Practise address	THE BACK BEDROOM, THOUGH I RUN A LENGTH OF GREEN GARDEN HOSE (B&Q) FROM THE BATHROOM. SO I SUPPOSE YOU MIGHT SAY BACK BEDROOM, BATHROOM AND LANDING. HOWEVER WE EMPTY BUCKETS INTO THE DOWNSTAIRS SINK.
Post/Area code	
Tel	
email	
mobile tel.	
website address	WWW.STANMADELEY.COM (COMING SOON!!!)
How long have you practised at this address	SINCE WE HAD IT REDECORATED IN MAY
Are you a full-time or part-time therapist? Please state	PART TIME
How long have you been practising colonic hydrotherapy?	3 WEEKS
Details of other qualifications. Please enclose photocopies of your certificates to support your application. 9 'O' LEVELS INCLUDING GRADE 'A' IN ENGLISH WITH DRAMA. 3 'A' LEVELS. A CABARET UNION GOLDEN 'ASKEY' FOR SERVICES TO CABARET. A CERTIFICATE IN 'HOME COLON HYDROTHERAPY' FROM THE STAR SPANGLED COLON COLONOSCOPY CLINIC -- AN INTENSIVE SIX WEEK DISTANCE LEARNING COURSE VIA THE INTERNET.	
List current Association memberships **CHAIRMAN OF THE BRITISH CABARET LEAGUE,** **PRESIDENT OF THE TORD GRIP GLEE CLUB**	

Section 3 – Professional Education

Name & Addresses and **telephone** numbers of study centre(s) where professional certificates gained, with dates of study. Please state whether full or part-time and length of course.

    The Star-Spangled College of the Colon
    Seckersville Ranch
    Utah
    29384

Name & Address and **telephone** number of study centre where Colonic Hydrotherapy course was taken, with dates(s). Please enclose photocopy of certificate.

    See attached certificate.

Other professional and academic qualifications

    Driving licence, library membership, 10% voucher from Boots, sticking plaster,
    Tesco clubcard, photo of wife Sandra (54), various credit cards, one train ticket
    to Nuneaton (void), receipt for an eel-skin wallet with 'Stan' stitched across corner.

Do you hold a current Appointed Persons' First Aid certificate? If so, please enclose a copy.
Please note you may submit your application without one, but it will be necessary to provide one for membership.

SECTION 4- Professional Indemnity Insurance & claims history

Please provide documentary evidence, including the name and contact details of your insurer, for minimum £2million professional indemnity cover and public liability cover. Please note, the ARCH block insurance scheme is only available to paid-up members in the UK, and is not valid until membership is granted. For overseas applicants, please send a photocopy of your cover certificate.

Have you had any claims made against you with respect your practice?	**YES** / NO
Are there any current claims outstanding against you?	**YES** / NO
Have you ever been party to civil proceedings related to your professional practice?	**YES** / NO
Have you ever had insurance refused or subject to loaded terms or increased premiums?	**YES** / NO
Have you ever been disciplined by a professional or regulatory body in the UK or overseas?	**YES** / NO
Have you ever been struck off any professional register?	**YES** / NO
Have you ever been convicted of a criminal offence in the UK, Europe or overseas?	**YES** / NO

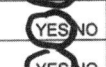

If you answer YES to any of the above, please give full details on a separate sheet.

SECTION 5 – Supporting Evidence

Please supply a detailed CV and a current colour photograph of yourself. Please attach. ✓

Please supply a resumé of how you became involved in complementary therapies and why you wish to join ARCH.

UK Only: Please supply **a subject access report**, under the Data Protection Act 1998 showing that you have not been prosecuted nor have a criminal Conviction. This is obtainable through your local police station (there is a fee payable for this) – take a means of identity and a recent utility bill with you.

It is a condition of membership that you do not have a criminal conviction. It is important for members of the public to be reassured that the colonic therapist has no relevant criminal convictions, especially relating to a sexual nature.

SECTION 6 – Declaration

I certify that the above information is correct. I agree to abide by the Constitution of the Association and Register of Colon Hydrotherapists, and to its Rules and Code of Ethics which will be sent upon processing of your application. I will advise ARCH of any change(s) in my status.

Signed: *[signature]*

Dated: 3/10/09

Membership fees - you will receive an invoice for this. **Do NOT send any money with this application.**

Document checklist:
This form completed and signed.
Copies of therapy certificates and/or current nursing registration
Copy of Colonic Hydrotherapy certificate
First Aid "Appointed Persons" certificate
Copy professional indemnity and public liability insurance certificate.
Detailed curriculum vitae.
Current Colour photograph of yourself (passport size or larger)
Resumé of your involvement in CAM and why you wish to join ARCH
Subject Access report from the Criminal Records Bureau.

Please return completed form and supporting documents to:

Abigail Francis,
ARCH Membership Secretary,

To: stan@stanmadeley.com
From: A. Francis
Date: 28/09/2009 15:07
Subject: re Application for membership of ARCH

Dear Stan

Thank you for your application to join ARCH. Before I can process your application I will need you to forward all the documents requested on the ARCH website eg a copy of your insurance, a current first aid certificate and of course a police check document.

I will pass you application to the chairman and the rest of the ARCH committee for appraisal, and possibly to the person who publishes our quarterly newsletter.

Yours sincerely

Abi Francis
Membership Secretary

:-)

STAN MADELEY
THE UK'S TOP RICHARD MADELEY LOOKALIKE
BM NOUMENON, LONDON, WC1N 3XX EMAIL: STAN@STANMADELEY.COM

Abigail Francis
Membership Secretary
Association and Register of Colon Hydrotherapists

5th October, 2009

Dear Ms. Francis,

Thank you for your email of 28/9/09. I must apologise for my not having returned the full application form. My pink tablets sometimes cause me to be forgetful.

On page 2 of the form, it asks for details of 'Professional Indemnity Insurance & Claims History'. If I may, I'll respond to those allegations here in this letter.

Have you had any claims made against you with respect to your practise?

Sadly, Abigail, I have. Mrs. Shaw (number 38) claimed that I'd deliberately turned the hose on 'jet' when she knew full well that it was still on 'vertical shower'. In my defence, Mrs. Shaw is a known troublemaker. Many people blame her for getting Trevor Sutcliffe thrown off the church bell-ringing team for clapper abuse.

Are there any current claims outstanding against you?

Mrs. Byswater claims she lost her earrings during a particularly thorough colonic session in the back bedroom. So far, we've been unable to find them. I'm going to lift the mattress and see if they've rolled under the bed but we're holding off until we get the vacuum fixed. We want to hoover under there since we have the chance.

Have you ever had insurance refused or subject to loaded terms or increased premiums?

My wife, Sandra (54), made a claim for damaged double glazing but they said it was caused by normal weather conditions and was therefore not covered.

Have you ever been disciplined by a professional or regulatory body in the UK or overseas?

I have been thrown out of the Magic Circle for inhumane treatment of a badger.

Have you ever been struck off any professional register?

See above regarding my badger. The RSPCA also got involved but I wasn't a member.

Have you ever been convicted of a criminal offence in the UK, Europe, or overseas?

I once killed a Barbary macaque on the Rock of Gibraltar. It was being particularly vicious, wrestling with my wife over an ice-cream cornet, so I picked it up by its tail and threw it over the cliff. The police charged me with murdering a gibbon and I was deported.

I trust this clears things up and that my application can now move forward like a well-lubricated nozzle.

Best wishes!

Whilst we're waiting for a reply, Sandra, could we look into buying a new nozzle?

← SANDRA (54) ← 17ft →

STAN MADELEY
THE UK'S TOP RICHARD MADELEY LOOKALIKE
BM NOUMENON, LONDON, WC1N 3XX   EMAIL: STAN@STANMADELEY.COM

Quentin Letts,　　　　　　　　　　　　　　　　　　　20th October, 2009
The Daily Mail
Associated Newspapers Limited
Northcliffe House, 2 Derry Street
London, W8 5TT

Dear Quentin,

In the highly unlikely chance you have yet to hear of me, please allow me to introduce myself. My name is Stanley Madeley (by deed poll) and I'm the UK's top Richard Madeley lookalike currently working the festival cabaret circuit with my surrealist one-man show, 'Dribbling Jaw Sack – The Stanley Madeley Experience Live!'.

Can I begin by saying how much I loved, admired, and plagiarised your book, *50 People Who Buggered Up Britain*, even if I didn't agree with all 55 of your choices. You included Jimmy Savile but not Jamie Oliver, which, quite frankly, seemed tantamount to listing Giscard d'Estaing among the people who buggered up Europe whilst ignoring the contributions made by an Austrian painter and decorator famously light in the underpants.

It's this tendency you have of 'missing the bigger picture' that has left me feeling obliged to write to you about the rise of extremists standing as independent candidates at the next general election. I know that you and your newspaper rightly make much about the threat posed by the BNP, but I can't help but feel that there are equally worrying individuals out there who are not getting the same exposure. For instance, I put it to you that you're not doing enough to combat the threat posed by Esther Rantzen.

I accept, Quentin, that you included her in the 'also rans' in the book's last chapter but do you really remember what it was like living through the dark days of the 1970s? Not only did the rubbish pile up on our streets but it piled up on our TVs too. Voters need reminding of the grim reality of That's Life Britain. Just imagine what will happen should Esther get power. Wit will be replaced by the tawdry innuendo that made me hostile to carrots for much of my adult life, and the world will be painted yellow, with soft furnishings on every hard surface, and the edges taken from all sharp instruments, including your pen.

She's already filling the newspapers with her filthy Luton propaganda. 'Luton is a vibrant, energetic, exciting, diverse place,' she says as though we'll believe it. But, Quentin, we know what she's really saying: 'Give me Luton and I'll give you the world!' This can only end badly; with Alan Titchmarsh as Foreign Secretary and the economy under the breasts of Nigella Lawson, though, to be honest, that might make the Budget a bit more watchable.

STAN MADELEY
THE UK'S TOP RICHARD MADELEY LOOKALIKE
BM NOUMENON, LONDON, WC1N 3XX   EMAIL: STAN@STANMADELEY.COM

Esther might portray herself as just a woman dressing younger than her age but I can't get over the news that she has her face injected with the grinning form of botulism. If you thought Tony Blair was the epitome of toothy sentimental chintz, wait until Rantzen gets into Number 10. It will be like being ruled by a gila monster dressed by Laura Ashley. David Icke will have a field day.

The next election will be extremely important in the history of this country. It's when we decide whether we abandon our national anthem for an irritating tuba-based theme song. I hope I can count on your support to stand in the way of this three-wheeled, democracy-crushing bandwagon built by Mothercare.

       Sincerely yours,

THE DAILY MAIL

Telegrams, Daily Mail, London, W.8.

Stan Madeley,
BM Noumenon,
London,
WC1N 3XX.

26 October 2009

Dear Stan,

Thank you for a corker of a letter. Much as I agree with you about Mother Rantzen, it is slightly tricky terrain for me as she is a great favourite of the paper.

Titchmarsh as Foreign Secretary? Well, he couldn't be worse than Miliband.

I return the glorious pic of Esther.

Best wishes,

Quentin Letts.

THE DAILY MAIL (A DIVISION OF ASSOCIATED NEWSPAPERS LTD.)

S T A N   M A D E L E Y
THE UK'S TOP RICHARD MADELEY LOOKALIKE
BM NOUMENON, LONDON, WC1N 3XX   EMAIL: STAN@STANMADELEY.COM

Matthew Parris
The Times
News International Limited
1 Virginia St, London

7th November, 2009

Dear Matthew,

Can I begin by saying that I have enjoyed your writing for many years? Your words are very important to me and, quite frankly, the only reason I consent to putting coins in Rupert Murdoch's purse. Allow me to introduce myself. My name is Stanley Madeley (by deed poll) and I'm the UK's top Richard Madeley lookalike, currently working in cabaret with my one-man show, 'Kiddies' Glockenspiel Furnace – The Stanley Madeley Experience Live!'.

I have just finished reading your fine article of November 7th, where you write that 'two big anxieties hang like dark clouds over the voters' minds this November'. One, you argue, is Afghanistan; the other, the collapse of our confidence in the parliamentary system. I think you underestimate a third concern. I write to ask you where you stand on the most pressing political question of our day: are you a 'Rantzen man' or will you stand behind me in my campaign to make Luton the most fiercely contested battleground of the next election?

As you might know, Ms. Esther Rantzen intends to stand as an independent candidate for Luton. I don't hold any grudge against the woman but I am trying to start a grass-roots movement against this country becoming a four-year-long episode of *That's Life*. I refuse to allow our national anthem to be replaced by a jaunty tune played on the tuba and I will not have parliamentary debate reduced to the level of oddly shaped vegetables. Frankly, Matthew, I do not want my Prime Minister addressing me from atop a kitchen stool whilst wearing a diaphanous purple gown and showing plenty of leg. We had enough of that with Tony Blair.

My fear is that Luton will not satisfy Esther for long. Before we know it, Alan Titchmarsh will be our Foreign Secretary and every hard edge in the country will be clad in feather pillows. We'll replace Belgium as Europe's laughing stock. Do you want Sweden mocking us for our government's policy of genitally clamping every man between the ages of 11 and 77? Do you want to live in a petting zoo for four years? A petting zoo containing nothing but rabbits with their fangs removed? Do you really want to be in bed for seven o'clock? It would happen under a Rantzen government.

So far, I've managed to get Quentin Letts on board but I feel that I need support from the broadsheets before I stand any chance of carrying the country in this vote. I will await your response, possibly in the form of a cleverly written 800-word column on this very subject.

Tipping you the wink,

Stan Madeley

From: Matthew Parris

The Times' Room,
House of Commons,
London SW1A 0AA

23rd November 2009

Dear Mr Madeley,

Thanks for your letter – it had me laughing out loud - and for your kind thought in enclosing a stamped addressed envelope for my reply.

Perhaps the occasion will arise in some future column to cull from it, but if not you have at least given me a lot of fun.

Yours sincerely,

Matthew Parris

Stanley Madeley, Esq.,
BM Noumenon,
London, WC1N 3XX

S T A N   M A D E L E Y
THE UK'S TOP RICHARD MADELEY LOOKALIKE
BM NOUMENON, LONDON, WC1N 3XX   EMAIL: STAN@STANMADELEY.COM

Bernie Clifton c/o
Michael Vine Associates
1 Stormont Road
London, N6 4NS

5th September, 2009

Dear Bernie (if I may),

Allow me to introduce myself. The name's Stan Madeley (by deed poll) and, as you can see, I pride myself on being the UK's top Richard Madeley lookalike. However, what you probably can't infer from my stationery is that, in my spare time, I breed ostriches. Yes, that's right: ostriches. I keep them on my own plot of land just outside Hastings.

I now own seventeen ostriches (Lucy, Raymond, Barney, Norris, Mabel, Hedgehog, Shaun, Withnail, Gordon, Barry, Lulu, Roger, Clive, Rambo, Cilla, Bernie and Bill) which my wife and I occasionally race locally at village fetes. They are a big hit with the children and simpletons, helping to raise money for charity. Last year alone, we raised £200 for the Kipping's Cross Owl Park, near Royal Tunbridge Wells.

Sadly, due to my wife unexpectedly giving birth to twins (I am not their father), I can no longer justify the expense of my ostriches and I write to you in advance of my packing my favourite ostrich (Cilla) into a crate and sending her to you gratis (which means: free of charge). I don't know your current situation (re. adequate ostrich space) but ostriches are amazingly docile birds that only require a couple of hours of attention each day. If you don't want to keep Cilla as a pet or use her as part of your excellent act, I would happily butcher her for you. Ostrich meat is much like turkey but without the high fat content. It goes particularly well with sprouts.

Tell me what you'd like me to do (with Cilla) and I will make the arrangements re. delivery / butchery.

Finally, would it be possible for my wife to have a signed photo? You once pecked her bottom in St. Helen's town centre (outside Superdrug). If only you'd been wearing your ostrich suit, it would have been forgivable. As it is, I think you're lucky she isn't pressing charges.

You remain, however, a legend in this house and, except for the late Tsar, there's no man, living or dead, whose signed picture we'd want more to adorn our wall.

Best wishes,

Bernie Clifton

Dear Stanley, I'm writing to you promptly in Sept. 09 but I bet you don't get it till January 2010 what with all the Bad Weather we'll probably get over Xmas and the Postal Strike etc. etc. so the delays not my fault.

Delighted to hear of your success with your Ostrich Herd, but be careful and give up before your back goes, (too late for me!). I would happily take some of your unwanted Birds but sadly we're full up here what with the Bad Weather (we'll be having) so good luck with your mission.

Excuse the Handwriting but Matron orders 'Lights Out' at teatime and I'm writing by candlelight.

Best Wishes
Bernie

Hope you like the P.C. & Poster

BERNIE CLIFTON

STAN MADELEY
THE UK'S TOP RICHARD MADELEY LOOKALIKE
BM NOUMENON, LONDON, WC1N 3XX EMAIL: STAN@STANMADELEY.COM

Right Reverend James Jones
Bishop's Lodge
Woolton Park
Liverpool, L25 6DT

4th September, 2009

Your Grace,

Allow me to introduce myself. My name is Stan Madeley (by deed poll) and I am the UK's top Richard Madeley impersonator and a twenty-year veteran of the cabaret circuit. Strange though this might sound, I am also a devout believer. I believe in the power of the soft-shoe shuffle and the morality of raising good cheer.

I'm not a man to beat about the burning bush so I'll get down to it: I needn't tell you that the world is in a sorry state. As soon as I heard of the tragic passing of Michael Jackson, I knew that somebody had to moonwalk into that void. Your Grace: I believe that 'we' are that man!

I propose that you join with me in a double act ('a veritable gala of showbiz and faith') as we tour the churches in your dioceses to spread the message that people should cheer up. Our act would be modelled on that of the great Flanders and Swann. I would ask you to play the piano while I stand front and centre, introduce the songs, and then sing the main lyric while Your Grace provides close harmony. Can you play the piano? Don't worry if you can't. I have a Casio WK-110 76 piano-style keyboard that my nephew can programme via his MIDI. As long as you move your fingers, it would fool anybody.

No doubt you have a few reservations. After all, you probably think that the scheme is bound to end in failure and/or ridicule. However, as it says in Hebrews 13:2 – 'Be not forgetful to entertain strangers: for thereby some have entertained angels unawares.' I have heard your voice and I'm positive it can entertain unaware angels anywhere. And you needn't worry about getting stage fright. If you freeze, I have developed a forty-five-minute stage act involving juggling, balloon animals, and amusing noises I can make in the back of my throat.

With Your Grace's permission, I'd like to send you a CD of my wife (technically, a baritone) singing all 150 psalms, reworked to popular show tunes. As you will hear, my plans are just the shot in the arm that the church needs in these profane days.

Hope you have not been too surprised by this offer and I look forward to your input into what is certain to be a fantastic project.

Blessings,

Stan Madeley

THE BISHOP OF LIVERPOOL

25th September, 2009

Stanley Madeley,
BM Boumenon,
London.
WC1N 3XX

Dear Stanley

I am sorry not to have replied sooner to you interesting letter and fascinating proposal. I have wanted to take some time to think about what you are proposing.

In spite of your confidence I am afraid that I simply do not see myself functioning in the very creative way which you have in mind. I am sorry to disappoint you and thank you very much for your thoughtfulness in approaching me.

God Bless you,

Yours sincerely,

+ Liverpool

STAN MADELEY
THE UK'S TOP RICHARD MADELEY LOOKALIKE
BM NOUMENON, LONDON, WC1N 3XX   EMAIL: STAN@STANMADELEY.COM

Supt Andrew Murray
Thames Valley Police
Kidlington Police Station
169-171 Oxford Road
Kidlington, OX5 2NU

16th January, 2009

Dear Superintendent Murray,

Just a quick note from a satisfied tax payer about the line you've taken with those officers of yours recently filmed for YouTube using their riot shields to toboggan down the snow-capped hills of Oxford. The newspapers quote you as saying that 'the snow has a habit of bringing out the child in all of us' and I thought those words very telling. I can read between the lines and you sound very much like a man after my own heart: all for a little discipline but happy to tip the lads a wink so they know where you really stand on the matter.

It was obvious to me that you had to be seen as the strict paterfamilias but I'm sure that we both recognise that there's nothing wrong with a few Whisky Tangos relieving the stresses of the criminal justice grind. Better a little bobsledding than losing their temper with some pimpled lout possessed by the scrumpy devil and lawyered up to his tattooed earlobes.

I often think that we've never had a Rodney King-type incident in this country because our police officers can relieve the stresses of their duties in ways that do no harm. When I was a lad, our local beat bobby used to drop in to see Mrs. Marsh at the end of the road. She was a widow and suffered terrible pangs of loneliness. Thankfully she had the constable, the milkman, the coalman, and Mr. Lewis at number 43 to help raise her spirits.

When I consider the types of people you and your officers have to deal with, I'm constantly surprised that you can remain as professional as you do. Hats off to you on that score! I'm firmly of the old school and believe that justice is sometimes best served away from the prying eyes of the YouTube generation.

Anyway, I thought I'd just send you a letter to say that you're all doing a fantastic job. If you or your officers ever want to bobsled on the riot shield bought with this taxpayer's money, I've now given you my permission in writing.

With you all the way,

Stan Madeley

Thames Valley Police

Supt Andrew Murray
LPA Commander - Oxford City

Mr Stanley Madeley
BM Noumenon
London
WC1N 3XX

Date: 8th March 2010

Dear Mr Madeley,

Firstly, my apologies for not responding sooner. I usually have quite a heavy in tray but the sledging escapade caused it to virtually collapse under the weight of correspondence from all four corners of the globe.

It was interesting to note the reaction of the public. The majority were very supportive of the officers but rather uncomplimentary to me. 'Grumpy Superintendent' was one of the kinder descriptions of me as a consequence of what they felt was an 'over the top quote'. There was also a significant minority of correspondents who were very angry that I had not taken the matter seriously enough and they appeared to want the officers publicly flogged!

This led me to believe I got the quote just about right and your letter was one of the very few that understood the fine line I was intending to tread between protecting the public purse and promoting the human side of policing and police officers.

The officers involved were a healthy mix of experience (Q.P.M included) and fresh out of the wrapper probationary constables. They all understand the power of the media but nevertheless were taken aback by their new found fame and 'notoriety'. They did well to take my advice and keep their heads down and let me take on the 'grumpy superintendent' tag.

They are, of course, a great bunch and I am very proud of service they give to the residents of Oxford. I am certain that should they need to use a riot shield in future they will be behind it rather than on it.

Thanks again for the letter.

Yours sincerely,

Supt Andrew Murray
LPA Commander – Oxford City

Serving with Pride and Confidence

```
S  T  A  N     M  A  D  E  L  E  Y
THE  UK'S  TOP  RICHARD  MADELEY  LOOKALIKE
BM NOUMENON, LONDON, WC1N 3XX    EMAIL: STAN@STANMADELEY.COM
```

Mr. Malcolm Walker CBE   9th March, 2010
Iceland Foods Plc
Second Avenue Deeside Industrial
Deeside, Flintshire, CH5 2NW

Dear Mr. Walker,

There have been many times over the last few years when wife and self have suffered frostbite in your freezers yet we have never once complained. Nor have we ever felt so left out in the cold as we do now.

We are extremely disappointed that we weren't given a chance to vote in the recent referendum. Then again, if we had, we would not have supported this brazen attempt to withhold the £2.4 billion that should rightly be in government coffers. It's bad enough that half my taxes have been used to support some dodgy banks without having the other half pocketed by you villains in the frozen-food industry. And as my wife, Sandra (54), put it this very morning: 'They might have had all that money off Alistair Darling but they still don't offer online shopping.'

Personally, I would also question the validity of any vote that sees an overwhelming 93% of your customers telling you that you shouldn't pay back the £2.4 billion your company owes to the British government. £2.4 billion! What on earth did you do with it? I sincerely hope you didn't use it to pay off that bloody awful Kerry Katona. Then again, Malcolm, isn't this precisely what happens when you mix with people like that? My skin used to crawl when that woman tried to sell me frozen prawns.

As you might know if you saw the recent BBC4 documentary about the British lookalike circuit, I have worked in cabaret for some fifteen years – the last six as the UK's top Richard Madeley lookalike. I can say with some confidence that I have come across some right chancers in my time but your company really takes the proverbial chocolate block. I've been locked out of my own dressing room by a Christmas elf who subsequently ran off with my trombone. I have caught my own agent embezzling the charitable foundation I set up to help save the Luton badger. I have even seen a night's box office takings disappear to Spain with a transgender theatre manager with an obsession with Alan Yentob. Yet the scale of your cheek is staggering.

However, I'm not writing to simply express my disgust but to offer a solution. Ten pence on a bag of peas. That's all it would take. It's not radical but it is doable. If you can shift 24,000,000,000 bags, this unfortunate situation will resolve itself.

I will end by saying that it is sad that you find yourself in this predicament but perhaps it will make you reconsider your approach to business. Never spend a punter's cash before they've bought a ticket: it's the golden rule of generations of vaudevillians and one you should emulate.

Sincerely yours,

To: stan@stanmadeley.com
From: Malcolm Walker <█████████████>
Date: 23/03/2010 14:32
Subject: Iceland

Who's Richard Madeley?

Is he that guy on daytime TV watched by the unemployed & bored housewives? I wonder how he can be impersonated.

Anyway, your misfortune might be to share a name with the guy. Ours is to share a name with the country but most people are intelligent enough to know there is no connection. When I started the business in 1970 my wife thought of the name & the only Icelandic person anyone had heard of at the time was Magnus Magnusson.

When we were a public company a bunch of Vikings bought shares in Iceland (they liked the name). Now we are private they are still our biggest shareholder except they went bust so the shares went to an Icelandic bank. Then they went bust so effectively the Icelandic government owns the shares. We are by far the most valuable asset the country owns & their plan is to sell their shares & use the money to pay back the British taxpayer.

I think your best plan is to keep shopping in Iceland as it's the only chance we Brits will have of ever getting repaid.

STAN MADELEY
THE UK'S TOP RICHARD MADELEY LOOKALIKE
BM NOUMENON, LONDON, WC1N 3XX   EMAIL: STAN@STANMADELEY.COM

Mr. Cooper   8th February, 2010
Managing Director
Armitage Shanks
Rugeley, Staffordshire
WS15 4BT

Dear Mr. Cooper,

In nearly seventeen years on the cabaret circuit, I have used bathroom fixtures of every shape, size, and colour. I have squatted and stood, balanced on one leg, two legs, and no legs. I have had to put up with every inconvenience of a bad convenience you can imagine. Yet in that time, I have also developed devices which any entertainer would be wise to use before going out on stage after a bathroom break. And it is with regard to one of these devices that I'm writing to you today. But please … Allow me to introduce myself. The name is Stanley Madeley (by deed poll) and I am the UK's top Richard Madeley lookalike and the inventor of the PD9.

What, you might ask yourself, is the PD9? Well, the PD9 is the ninth prototype of the device that will save gentlemen from one of the most common problems with visiting the bathroom.

Picture the scene: you're in a business meeting. It's the height of summer so you're wearing your cream chino casuals with socks and sandals. Being sensible, you have been drinking plenty of water but now your bladder is full. You need to visit the bathroom. You excuse yourself then off you go to the gents, which is no doubt outfitted in Armitage Shanks' range of the quality porcelain and stainless. You stand at the urinal, your mind on other things as you relieve yourself. Perhaps you whistle a cheerful song. Suddenly you remember that you've not mentioned the excited growth forecast for outdoor plumbing supplies. Eager to get back to the meeting, you quickly tap yourself off and zip yourself up.

And that's when crisis strikes! You feel that sensation dreaded my men everywhere. Residual moisture is now running down your leg. Down your thigh it goes, across your inner knee, and down your shin until it meets your sock. At the very least, you'll have the stigma of the damp patch sitting to the side of your zip (right or left, depending on how you dress).

Faced with this predicament, you might try to use paper towels or stand in front of the hand dryer with the nozzle jammed down your waistband. But we all know that won't work! You are instead forced to pull down your shirt to cover the patch or walk backwards into the boardroom. But that doesn't work either. Everybody can see what has happened and no exciting growth forecasts for external plumbing supplies can alter the fact that you're now the laughing stock of the industry.

STAN MADELEY
THE UK'S TOP RICHARD MADELEY LOOKALIKE
BM NOUMENON, LONDON, WC1N 3XX   EMAIL: STAN@STANMADELEY.COM

However, with the PD9, residual spillage is no longer a problem. Based around spacecraft technology, I have devised a high-pressure jet of air that shoots up your trouser leg and dries you from crotch to ankle in seconds. It's quick. It's efficient. And, what's more, it's fun! And I would be delighted to come and demonstrate it for you at the earliest convenience (pun intended).

What if I say the morning of the 24th March at 10.30AM? Remember, I'm coming to you before I go to your competitors!

Fully dry down there,

[signature]

PS. I have fully patented the concept so don't get any ideas!

To: stan@stanmadeley.com
From: John Hardy
Date: 09/03/2010 12:11
Subject: your letter to Mr Cooper our MD

Dear Mr Madeley, firstly please let me apologise for the length of time it has taken to respond to your letter – initially I have to confess opinion was split whether you were being serious or whether we were part of a script for a new gag in your latest routine. I'm sure most, if not all men would recognise the embarrassing scenario you describe – maybe that's why dark suits still remain popular as the evidence is harder to spot. I don't think however that we are in a position to take advantage of your invention. Our expertise is in Ceramics and associated plumbing – we don't have any experience in air blowers or dryers. I think maybe the Dyson organisation might be a better potential partner. Thanks for thinking of us and good luck with developing your idea – I look forward to it becoming available!!!

STAN MADELEY
THE UK'S TOP RICHARD MADELEY LOOKALIKE
BM NOUMENON, LONDON, WC1N 3XX   EMAIL: STAN@STANMADELEY.COM

Dr. Sarah Elton
Mammal Ecology and Environments Group
Hull York Medical School
Cottingham Road
Hull, HU6 7RX

7th February 2010

Dear Dr. Elton,

I don't suppose you have much contact with the world of cabaret but I find myself in the unusual position of needing your help on a matter of great importance. Allow me to introduce myself. The name is Stanley Madeley (by deed poll) and, like you, I am fascinated by Old World monkey palaeobiology!

The gig is simple. My wife, Sandra (54), has decided that she is tired of being the Judy in my Richard Madeley lookalike act. I suppose that the years of standing still in the chisel-throwing finale have finally got to her. Naturally, I want to support her in any way that I can. She has chosen to branch out (pun intended) into the world of performing monkeys and she has arranged with a local businessman to import some baboons into the country. Don't ask me for details because, to be perfectly honest, Sarah, I know very little of the process or where they come from. It was a cash-up-front arrangement and I only know that the baboons will be arriving in April or May.

The problem we now face is that we have been unable to find anybody in the UK who knows much about training a baboon. Let me just calm the fears you will undoubtedly have at this point. There are no animal rights issues to worry about. We are fully prepared to house the baboons in a healthy environment (we have a spare back bedroom) and with the proper food and sanitation (we are plumbed both upstairs and down). Where we are lacking is in our training regimen. In short, how do we teach them the tricks?

We were thinking it would be easiest if we started out with the old staples: riding a tricycle, smoking a cigarette, and then dancing à la John Travolta in *Saturday Night Fever*. My wife is in the process of hand-stitching a disco-style white suit that will fit a baboon from collar to cuff. From there, we would hopefully get the baboons tumbling, performing rudimentary gags, and, finally, interacting with each other. Her ambition is to have them able to act out a drama set around the Nick Cave song, 'Stagger Lee', set inside a fully scaled-down baboon bar. A baboon barkeeper would stand polishing glasses, another would play 'Stagger Lee' complete with sidearm, and then assorted baboons would play dead on command in a choreographed orgy of violence and bananas.

Listen, I could carry on setting the scene but I'm sure that you've already got some good ideas. Allow me to simply finish by thanking you for your time and by saying that I very much look forward to your reply and your future involvement in what should be an exciting new act in the world of late-night cabaret.

Old World monkeys are the best!

SARAH ELTON.

3rd June 2010

HYMS

THE HULL YORK
MEDICAL SCHOOL
Tel 0870 1245350

HULL
The University of Hull
Hull
HU6 7RX
Fax 01482 464705

YORK
The University of York
Heslington
York
YO10 5DD
Fax 01904 321696

www.hyms.ac.uk

Dear Stanley,

Thank you for your letter dated 7th February 2010. Apologies for the length of time it has taken to get back to you.

English translation:

Dear Stanley,

Thank you for your letter dated 7th February 2010. Apologies for the length of time it has taken to get back to you.

I would caution about offering the cigarettes, especially prior to the Travolta-style routines. It tends to make the baboon cough, which disrupts the rhythm. But the tricycle is a great idea – much easier than the unicycle my research group was working on with vervet monkeys.

Baboons hate Nick Cave (and who can blame them?). Independent peer-reviewed research has found however that they love 1980s hair metal, especially Bon Jovi.

Hope this helps to refine the routine, and best of luck – hope the monkeys are comfortable in the back bedroom.

All the best, Sarah.

STAN MADELEY
THE UK'S TOP RICHARD MADELEY LOOKALIKE
BM NOUMENON, LONDON, WC1N 3XX   EMAIL: STAN@STANMADELEY.COM

The British Historical Games Society 15th September, 2009
8 West Hill Avenue
Epsom
Surrey, KT19 8LE

Dear Sir/Madam,

Allow me to introduce myself. My name is Stanley Madeley (by deed poll) and I am the UK's top Richard Madeley lookalike with over fourteen years of experience of the cabaret circuit. I am also a fanatical wargame enthusiast and intend to use my high public profile to launch a new miniature-based set that I designed around the Siege of Harlech Castle.

As you probably know, the siege was the longest in UK history, lasting seven years, thus making it perfect for tabletop re-enactment. I have designed a 1:100 scale replica of Harlech Castle and reached an agreement with a reputable Taiwanese manufacturer to produce them at a reasonable price (£16 a turret, no less!). As I type, there are 5,000 Harlech Castles sitting on a dock in Kaohsiung.

I have designed a series of rules for the game, including a complicated system of resupplying from the sea. In addition, players have the ability to lower defensive scores by firing diseased sheep carcasses into the fort using my patented miniature sheep-catapults, also being manufactured in Taiwan and also sitting on a Far East dock.

This brings me to my reason for writing. I have failed to find any 1:100-scale replica sheep and lack the funds to have them manufactured. Since they are so central to the game – indeed, the sheep are the game's greatest novelty – I wondered if you or any member of your society would know of a place I could source them. If you can't find sheep, other livestock would do, though diseased is preferable and anything as small as a chicken would probably look ridiculous. Goats would be ideal. In exchange, anybody who can source me my sheep will receive one of the first Harlech Castles to reach the country.

I would like to end by thanking you for your time and the work you put into the world of historical games. When my surrealist one-man show, 'Lime Green Napoleon — The Stanley Madeley Experience Live', recently took me to Manchester, I had chance to attend 'Britcon 2009' in the wonderfully named Barnes Wallis Building (though I wish it was engineered to his high standards!). I had a simply fantastic time and my enjoyment was most certainly at the 1:1 scale! Well done to all who organised the event and I hope to see you all again in the near future.

Your most humble servant,

Stanley ('3 shots if immobile') Madeley

To: stan@stanmadeley.com
From: J.D. McNeil
Date: 22/09/2010 08:21
Subject: BHGS

Hi Stan

You wrote to me at BHGS regarding your visit to Britcon. Glad you enjoyed it.

Re your Harlech Castle project I think Irregular Miniatures might be your answer. They do a range of 15mm and 25mm farm animals, so I would give that a try.

I am writing to you from my business e-mail address as it occurred to me that our web store at www.playhistory.net might be worth looking at it if you are looking for an outlet to sell your project.

Slitherine as you might know are publishers and developers of video games and the Field of Glory Wargames rules but we also support businesses that are ancillary to our core business. See our various web site addresses below.

Take a look and if interested drop me a line

Best of luck with the project

Regards

JDM

```
S T A N   M A D E L E Y
THE UK'S TOP RICHARD MADELEY LOOKALIKE
BM NOUMENON, LONDON, WC1N 3XX   EMAIL: STAN@STANMADELEY.COM
```

Mr. Kipling
Fish Dam Lane
Carlton Barnsley
S71 3HQ

4th September 2009

Dear Mr. Kipling,

Allow me to introduce myself. My name is Stan Madeley (by deed poll) and I am the UK's top Richard Madeley impersonator. You may have heard of me. I have just finished touring South Yorkshire with my surrealist one-man show, 'Cheap Garrotted Spaniel – The Stanley Madeley Experience Live'.

I've been a fan of your work for many, many years. To say that you've made me the man I am is an understatement. Nobody has meant more to me in a non-religious or non-sexual way than your good self.

If you'll permit me, I have written a poem to express all that you mean to me, borrowing the lines from one of your very own poems, but reflecting your well-known fondness for cakes. I hope you like it. I worked on it for nearly 30 minutes last Sunday afternoon.

If (v. 2.0)
by Stanley Madeley

If you can stuff your mouth when all about you
Are stuffing theirs, annoying you with their chew,
If you can eat an almond slice or maybe two,
But polish off an apple tart for pudding too;
If you can eat flan, and then, tired by waiting,
Or being lied to by men about French Fancies,
Or being sated, do you just carry on eating,
And yet don't look too good, nor talk too wise?
Yours is the sponge pudding and everything that's in it,
And – craving more – you'll be fat, my son!

I hope you enjoyed the poem. I have ten others that are equally impressive, including a poem about the Siege of Mafeking based around the Battenberg. Would you like to read them?

If it's not too much to ask, could you please sign the photo I've included. If you make it out 'To dearest Stan', I will be forever grateful.

Kindest regards,

[signature]

PREMIER FOODS

Our Ref: 12399
8 September 2009

→ *The point at which the letter runs into the document's header, making it very hard to read the date or the reference number, especially for people with vision difficulties and/or colour blindness.*

Mr Madeley
Bm Noumenon
London
WC1N 3XX

Dear Mr Madeley

Thank you for your letter with regard to Mr Rudyard Kipling and The range of Mr Kipling cakes that we make.

I am sure you can appreciate that the two names are not connected at all and the one associated with the cakes that we make is not a real person. Mr Kipling exists in the hearts and minds of Manor Bakerie's and Premier Foods employees and all cake lovers. He was created over 30 years ago to represent the exceedingly good cakes the company was producing and now encapsulates everything the brand stands for, and personifies what is good about the company - its vision, its values and insistence on quality.

I wish you well with your tour and show and thank you for taking the time and trouble to write to me.

Yours sincerely

Kevin Moseley
Customer Care Manager

Manor Bakeries, Fish Dam Lane, Barnsley, South Yorkshire S71 3HQ Tel: +44 (0)1226 286791 Fax: +44 (0)1226 291003
Premier Grocery Products Limited. Registered in England Number 1644110. Registered Office: Premier House, Centrum Business Park, Griffiths Way, St Albans, Hertfordshire AL1 2RE

STAN MADELEY
THE UK'S TOP RICHARD MADELEY LOOKALIKE
BM NOUMENON, LONDON, WC1N 3XX   EMAIL: STAN@STANMADELEY.COM

Mr. Kevin Moseley
Customer Care Manager
Manor Bakeries / Mr. Kipling's
Fish Dam Lane
South Yorkshire S71 3HQ

23rd September, 2009

Re. Your Reply and Tarts

Dear Mr. Moseley,

I needn't introduce myself. You might remember that I wrote to you recently with a poem intended for Mr. Kipling. You proceeded to explain that he doesn't exist and that he is actually a figment of my imagination. You passed no comment on my poem.

Despite that, your reply was certainly generous and it cleared things up considerably, even if it did cause both my wife and self some days of heartache, if not mourning. But be that as it may, I am now writing with regard to your reply. Despite her tears, my ever astute wife, Sandra (54), was the first to point out that you had printed your letter *over* the header of your stationery. I have included a photocopy of the letter, indicating where the mishap occurred. As you can see, the reference number and date are barely legible, hence the reason why I can quote neither to you now.

When I saw this, I was, quite frankly, shocked. I wondered what kind of semi-professional operation you're running up there on Fish Dam Lane. What, I thought, if you'd been applying the same sloppy work practices to your baking? I had to investigate.

I proceeded to purchase two (2) boxes of your Mr. Kipling's Bakewell Tarts (see figure 1) and it was as I suspected! Your cherries do not line up! Despite the perfect alignment of the cherries on the picture on the box, the cherries inside can be off-centre by anything up to a centimetre (see figure 2) on both the vertical and horizontal axes. In my sample of twelve (12) tarts, I found only one aligned centrally and that was a 'split cherry' which had broken in two.

I have worked fifteen years on the cabaret circuit and if I'd been as lax in my duties as you have been in placing cherries on your tarts, then I would never have placed a single showgirl's tassel in the middle of her pert breast. Now, you might be tempted to say that my 'tarts' were luckier than yours, Mr. Moseley, but such a joke would be beneath me and demean the seriousness of this issue.

Anyway, I hope you appreciate that I've gone to some considerable time and expense in undertaking this study on behalf of Mr. Kipling. I would have that you treat this letter seriously and pass it on to the department in charge of cherry placement. I thank you again for your letter, shoddily printed though it was.

Sincerely yours,

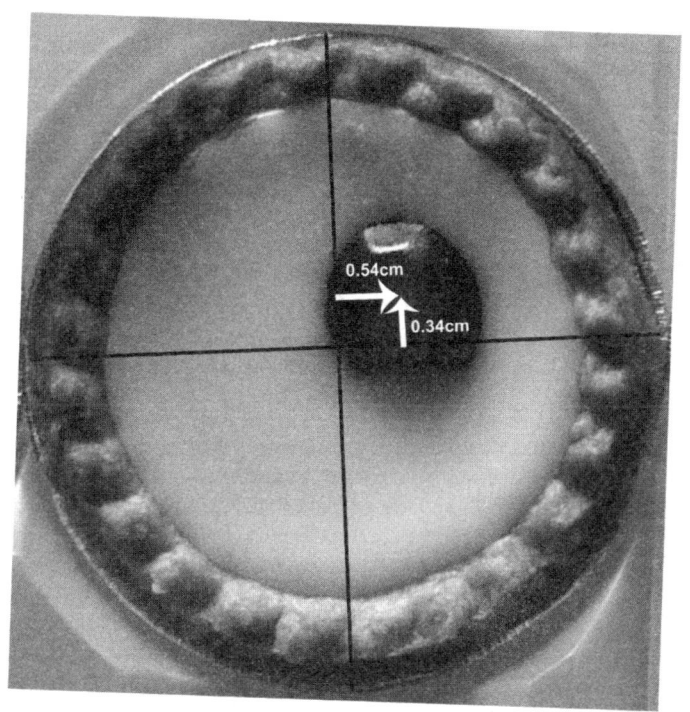

Figure 2. The measured displacement of a single cherry on one of our 12 sample Kipling's Bakewell tarts. Measurements established by use of micrometer.

Remind me to write to Mr. Kipling <u>himself</u> to tell him about this shoddy lack of a reply!

STAN MADELEY
THE UK'S TOP RICHARD MADELEY LOOKALIKE
BM NOUMENON, LONDON, WC1N 3XX EMAIL: STAN@STANMADELEY.COM

The Vegan Society
Donald Watson House
21 Hylton Street
Hockley, Birmingham
B18 6HJ

4th September, 2009

All Hail, Fellow Vegans!

Allow me to introduce myself. My name is Stanley Madeley (by deed poll) and I am the UK's top Richard Madeley lookalike, having worked the cabaret circuit for the past 15 years.

Don't worry if a cynical smile has just appeared about your lips. I'm more than used to people's scorn. I have faced cynicism throughout my life, but especially when it comes to my claiming to be a Vegan.

It's why I felt compelled to write to you. When I noticed your address in the local newspaper, I finally realised that I was not alone. With all the jokes and snorts of disgust I've endured through my life, I've found it hard to live as a Vegan in the modern world. I can't even sit down to lunch without having my tastes considered alien and a thing to be mocked. I'm sure you too have had to face the catcalls of non-Vegans, to whom our ways seem an affront to their very existence. It is sad when the very progress of human civilisation has been a matter of casting aside outmoded customs and what seemed normal to one age is cruel and barbaric to another. Shame on these heathens for not realising that we are so much more advanced than they!

Finding your address and writing to you has finally brought closure to all that I have suffered. I just wanted to thank you for making me feel no longer lost in this alien world. I am now so very content in the knowledge that when the mothership lands and we return to Vega, these humans will laugh no more.

Paldo spa ingloria na midgera,

[signature]

Must be those reclusive Vegans from over in the asteroid belt. Good job they didn't reply. They'd only bore us with stories of space dust.

Daily Mail, Friday, January 1, 2010   Page 65

QUESTION: What is the fate of the nation's liposuction fat?

FURTHER to the earlier answer, my wife Sandra has run a liposuction clinic in South-West London for the past 25 years.

In the early days, I was closely involved in the disposal of the fat during the liposuction process.

I cannot confirm the popular urban myth, perpetuated by the film Fight Club, that liposuction can be used to make soap and explosives. The price of liposuction fat has certainly dropped significantly in recent years since the introduction of new government guidelines as to its disposal.

The current practice is to box it up and arrange to have it picked up by a medical waste company to be incinerated. However, up to about ten years ago, we would often sell liposuction fat as a heavy lubricant for marine use. Nautical friends claimed that human fat was the best way to grease their prop shafts.

We have also sold our fat for uses including the manufacture of bowler hats and as an ingredient in loam.

Long-distance swimmers (including many who swam the Channel) swore by the insulation provided by our fat, which provides a better thermal barrier to cold sea water than the more customary goose fat.

At the time, I found this anecdote most amusing as it reminded me of Robert Burton's description of authors who 'lard their lean books with the fat of others' works'. As far as I know, liposuction fat has never been used in cooking.

Stanley Madeley, London WC1.

Great result, Sandra, but I'm disappointed they didn't publish my explanation of the uses of custard in the space program.

STAN MADELEY
THE UK'S TOP RICHARD MADELEY LOOKALIKE
BM NOUMENON, LONDON, WC1N 3XX   EMAIL: STAN@STANMADELEY.COM

Carol Gorton
Arnold Bennett Society
4 Field End Close
Stoke on Trent
ST4 8DA

4th September, 2009

Dear Ms. Gorton,

Allow me to introduce myself. My name is Stanley Madeley (by deed poll) and, as you can see, I am the UK's top Richard Madeley lookalike. I work mainly in cabaret throughout the UK but also perform acts of charity on behalf of owl hospices in the Norfolk region. I am also a HUGE fan of Mr. Bennett's work.

May I say how absolutely delighted I was to discover, via a vocal artiste friend of mine (Ruby Prune), that there was a society in honour of my favourite tragedian. I have been an admirer for many years and would love to join (if the price is reasonable).

Could you also tell me if there are any annual trips or jaunts planned to celebrate Mr. Bennett's work? Indeed, would it be possible to visit the Great Man, or to write to him with questions that he could answer at his leisure?

Also, is there a discount membership scheme for married couples? It was my wife, Sandra (54), who first introduced me to Mr. Bennett's work. I remember the joy I felt when she treated me to tickets to see *A Question of Attribution* at the Hastings Playhouse in 1992. If you would like, I can write some pieces for your newsletter. Or if you don't have a newsletter, I'd be delighted to create one for you using my Desktop Publishing Package. In fact, it would be an absolute pleasure. I have some clip art of some savoury snacks that I could use to recreate the famous 'Cream Cracker Under the Settee' incident as enacted by the much-missed Dame Thora.

I look forward to your response and will now rush off and reread some of my favourite dramatic monologues in anticipation of your reply.

May I finally add that this is all so very exciting!

Kind regards,

Arnold Bennett Society

To promote the study and appreciation of the life, works and times, not only of Arnold Bennett himself, but also of other provincial writers, with particular relationship to North Staffordshire.

5th September 2009

Mr Stan Madeley,
BM Noumenon
London
WC1N 3XX

Dear Mr Madeley,

Thank you for your letter of 4th September. But I believe you have the wrong "Bennett".

Mr Arnold Bennett was born in 1867 and died in 1931. He was a novelist, playwright, essayist, critic and journalist.

While **Mr Alan Bennett** is a great writer, he is not in **Mr Arnold Bennett's** league. If you Google "Arnold Bennett" you will find hours of reading about this great Victoria/Edwardian writer, who continues to be mentioned in national newspapers. Just today, in the Guardian and The Times, contained in two obituaries to Mr Keith Waterhouse who passed away yesterday at the age of 80 - another great writer - you can find quotes by **Mr Arnold Bennett**.

The current Arnold Bennett society was reformed in 1954 and has over 300 members worldwide. A more recent member is Mr Gyles Brandreth. Our annual dinner attracts such speakers as David Suchet, A N Wilson, Deborah Moggach, and Roy Hattersley.

If you would like more information about becoming a member of the society, please go to our website listed below.

Very best wishes

Carol A Gorton
Carol Gorton,
Secretary.

STAN MADELEY
THE UK'S TOP RICHARD MADELEY LOOKALIKE
BM NOUMENON, LONDON, WC1N 3XX EMAIL: STAN@STANMADELEY.COM

Robert Walker
Chairman, WH Smith PLC
180 Wardour Street
London, W1F 8FY

23rd September, 2009

Re. Rabbits

Dear Mr. Walker,

Please allow me to introduce myself. My name is Stanley Madeley (by deed poll) and, as you might know, I am the UK's top Richard Madeley lookalike, currently appearing across the country in my one-man show, 'The Stanley Madeley Experience Live!'. What you probably don't know is that, in my day job, I am a self-employed business trouble shooter. I like to invest in people and I believe that I bring added value to the companies I advise.

However, let me begin by laying the background to my reason for writing. For the past fifteen years, my wife, Sandra (54), has worked as a teacher in a state secondary school. Most evenings, she is marking work until around 9 or 10 o'clock at night, so I spend most of my time surrounded by the imaginative output of the minds of 11 to 16-year-olds. I pretty much know what's going on in their lives and the kinds of things they enjoy. And this gives me great insight as to what would sell.

I've noticed, for example, that many young girls seem happiest when drawing rabbits coloured in a garish pink. Part of the reason for this, I suppose, is because your company cleverly markets stationery branded with the Playboy logo. I don't know about you, Mr. Walker, but I'd feel pretty proud of myself that 12- and 13-year-old girls are growing up with a positive attitude towards pornography. It's so refreshing that a high street brand, respected as a family-friendly company, should also quietly go about changing attitudes towards the greased buttock and the dewy nipple. Bravo, sir! However, I think we're missing a fantastic opportunity to indoctrinate (I believe that's the right word) children with other core brands in the happy, glamorous world of adult pornography.

What I propose, sir, is that you begin to sell stationery branded with the trademarks of *Hustler*, *Mayfair*, and *Asian Wives*. This is your chance to change the attitudes of a new generation to magazines that have been wrongly reviled by certain moralising sections of the media. You've done an excellent job by helping to turn the Playboy Bunny into an icon of chavish fashion, so why can't we do the same with 'Razzle'?

Indeed, I think it is particularly edifying that their pocket-money should be directed into the Playboy Empire, who can use it to make more excellent TV viewing such as 'Rear Pleasures', 'Portrait of a Lesbian' and 'Sophie's Wet Dreams'. Sir, I commend the work your company has been doing and I hope you continue to fight the good fight for bad-living roués and libertines everywhere!

Warmest regards,

[signature]

From Kate Swann
Group Chief Executive

WH Smith PLC

180 Wardour Street
London W1F 8FY

5 October 2009

Telephone (0207) 851 8800
Facsimile   (0207) 851 8847

Mr S Madeley
BM Noumenon
London   WC1N 3XX

Dear Mr Madeley

Thank you for your recent letter which I am responding to in the absence of Mr Walker who is currently away from the office.

As one of the UK's leading retailers of books, magazines, newspapers and entertainment products, we aim to offer our customers choice, whilst also respecting customer views.

Customers often have strongly differing views about the products we sell, so we aim to strike the right balance to meet the needs of all our customers whilst not acting as a censor.

We believe that our customers should choose the products they buy – be it magazines, newspapers, DVDs, music, multimedia games or books. We always take into account the level of knowledge, sophistication and maturity of the people we are marketing to, particularly children. Our Marketing Code of Practice sets out the standards we will follow in our promotional activity, marketing and advertising.

Our ranges reflect current consumer trends and include a number of brands that will appeal to each age group, so they can make a choice based on their individual tastes.

We constantly add or remove ranges based on customer research, sales and customer feedback. Many products go in and out of fashion and require updating. From data received we concluded in January of this year that it was time to change the Playboy range and therefore whilst we sold through the remaining stock, no new orders were placed and therefore the range has been discontinued in our stores.

I hope you will agree that it is important for us to cater for customers with different views and preferences and not to act as a censor or limit choices.

Yours sincerely,

Kate Swann

cc Robert Walker

STAN MADELEY
THE UK'S TOP RICHARD MADELEY LOOKALIKE
BM NOUMENON, LONDON, WC1N 3XX   EMAIL: STAN@STANMADELEY.COM

Daniel Corbett   27th November, 2009
Weatherman
BBC Weather Centre
Wood Lane, London

Dear Mr. Corbett, or if you'll allow me, Daniel,

Allow me to introduce myself. My name is Stanley Madeley (by deed poll) and I am highly sought after as a Richard Madeley lookalike. I also work in cabaret throughout the South East in my own one-man show. Yet, if you'll forgive me, I am not writing about my professional life. I am writing about the effect you have on my 103-year-old grandmother, Milly.

When you first appeared on our screens, my Nanna had yet to reach her century. Yet still how she feared you! You would pause in the middle of your beautifully constructed weather reports, turn to camera, and say something like: 'It's perfect weather for giving your dear old grandmother a jolly trip out.' She would respond as you might imagine an elderly grandmother might: with abject terror! She believed you were telling us to get her out of the house and into a nursing home. Every evening's weather forecast would give us cause to wonder if we'd have to coax Nanna Milly out of the linen cupboard because of your poorly chosen words.

After a few years, she calmed down and now she doesn't take your 'threats' half so seriously. In fact, she has quite taken a shine to you, Daniel, and will often cheer when you appear and offer little taunts of her own. 'Such a lovely man,' she will say. 'Oh! My barometric pressure's rising! I'd get wet with him any time he likes!'

As you can see, my grandmother can be a touch vulgar. Indeed, it is sad to say that her vulgarity is becoming a little too much to handle with young children in the house. And here, I'm afraid, Daniel, I come to my purpose for writing. We are now in a position where we would like to put Milly in a retirement home but we lack the heart to tell her. Do you think it would be possible, during one of your longer forecasts for the Six O'Clock News, to turn to the camera and say: 'Wonderful weather to take your grandmother to a lovely little home where they enjoy jelly for tea every night'? This would provide a point at which my wife could segue into explaining the situation to Milly and for the rest of us to get the car loaded with her things before she even notices.

I really hope you can help us out: this is your chance, Daniel, to make amends.

Finally, permit me to end by thanking you for your attention and for bringing such drama to the weather forecast. You are our favourite. And all I believe that leaves me to do is to point in your general direction and say 'and that's your letter . . . for now!'

                    Sincere best wishes,

PS. If you could send us a signed photo, it might be a handy way of luring Milly into the car. It's either that or we'll have to lace her cocoa with gin.

To Milly Best wishes from Daniel Corbett

British Broadcasting Corporation Roon 2027 Television Centre Wood Lane London W12 7RJ
Telephone +44(0)20 8743 8000 Fax +44(0)20 8749 2864 Email weather@bbc.co.uk

BBC

The BBC Weather Centre

Dear Stanley

Thankyou for your letter and kind words. I hope you have managed to coax Milly to her new home!

regards
Daniel Corbett.

With Compliments

INVESTOR IN PEOPLE

STAN MADELEY
THE UK'S TOP RICHARD MADELEY LOOKALIKE
BM NOUMENON, LONDON, WC1N 3XX   EMAIL: STAN@STANMADELEY.COM

Sir David Attenborough
████████████
████████████
████████████

8th December, 2009

Dear Sir David,

Wife (Sandra, 54) and self are just back from a ten-mile hike through England's green and pleasant and I had a sudden urge to do something monumentally patriotic but with an environmental slant. It was a choice between knitting a Union Jack twitching tent for Bill Oddie or writing to the nation's top naturalist. I handle words better than I do wool so QED.

The fact is, Sir David, I'm a troubled man. Sea levels rising, species going extinct by the hour, apocalyptic droughts sweeping across Africa, America, and Australia, Esther Rantzen running for parliament … The world is in a sorry mess. (Happy Christmas, by the way! Card enclosed.) It makes me wonder if the last century of technological progress was really worth it. Don't get me wrong: my regard for Charles Darwin is almost as high as my regard for your good self. And I have no problem being related to the apes. Sandra's side of the family have good hearts but they do have a certain dexterity about their feet that just isn't natural.

But the way I feel about it, Science has become a fetish to some, a bandwagon to others. And the problem with bandwagons (as well as some fetishes) is that people tend to fall from the back of them. The media treat Science as though it is Celebrity's less interesting sister. I'm probably an exception. My carbon footprint is smaller than that of a dwarf in stiletto heels. However, to Dick and Anthea Suburban-4x4-Washing-Machine, Science gives them the right to abdicate all their responsibilities. Science is the answer to all of life's problems; an arrogant god with all the smart remarks. Which is why I believe that broadcasters have a duty to portray the true humility of Science.

Without this sense of humanity – a quality that you personified in your decades of broadcasting – TV documentaries are beginning to lack soul. They're just a marketing opportunity and a chance for some rum cove of a celebrity to plug a book and nab themselves a free holiday at the licence-payer's expense. What does Bear Grylls teach us about our natural world by sucking the juice from a dead yak's eyeball? Or Michaela Strachan, frolicking with a chimp? I'm sure she's a lovely girl and that the baboons adore her, but this requirement that a documentary be hosted by a celebrity is just plain wrong. Bring back Bellamy, is what I say!

I notice that Titchmarsh has been nosing his way into the natural history gig. But where's the lifetime of dedication? Our universities must have at least one or two experts who can read an autocue and don't look like a squashed pug. I have no problem with the BBC's staff behind the camera. Top notch men and women, the lot. It's the types we're getting in front of cameras that put me off. If Stephen Fry tells me to go out and save the racoon, there's no more certain way to make me wear a coonskin hat within the week.

Your friend in cabaret,

[signature]

16.12.09

Dear Stan Madeley

I agree with you about the importance of programmes a science. May I suggest that you let the BBC know your views

Yours,

David Attenborough

from Sir David Attenborough OM CH FRS

STAN MADELEY
THE UK'S TOP RICHARD MADELEY LOOKALIKE
BM NOUMENON, LONDON, WC1N 3XX EMAIL: STAN@STANMADELEY.COM

H.R.H. The Prince of Wales
Clarence House
St James's Palace
London, SW1 1BA

7th November, 2009

Your Royal Highness,

Since I am yet to have the pleasure of bending my balloons for you at a Royal Variety Performance, please allow me to introduce myself. The name is Stanley Madeley (by deed poll) and I am the UK's top Richard Madeley lookalike, currently working in cabaret with my hit one-man show 'Aluminium Thrusting Pole – The Stanley Madeley Experience Live!'.

Sir, I've stood back long enough but now feel that I can't keep my heels to the skirting any longer! What on earth is going on with Trafalgar Square? If it's not statues of ordinary people, it's ordinary people pretending to be statues.

You see, sir, there are many men in this country who share your cynicism towards modernism, postmodernism, or, as my wife, Sandra (54), likes to call it, 'that pretentious bloody rubbish'. This is why I have taken the liberty of contacting you. Not only did I want to give you the 'thumbs up' and say 'carry on' for the great stand you have made against the rising tide of intellectual guff, but I thought I'd lay out a few ideas which I believe haven't been brought to your attention.

What I propose is simple. Celebrating war heroes is fine to a point, but what about celebrating people who bring joy into our lives? We need a national monument to comedy and who better to represent the nation's funny men than The Goons? I have the photograph in mind; quite a famous one of the four of them (naturally, I include the great Michael Bentine!) acting the fool around a microphone. Cast in bronze, it would make a popular tourist attraction and prove that we care as much about our comedians as we do our warriors.

Now, I'm not strong on organisation. And, to tell you the truth, I haven't got much experience in casting bronze. But I'm sure that you do. Sir, allow me to suggest that you lead the project. I'm sure you need only sniff the name Milligan, nod towards the vacant plinth in T. Square, and people would be all over the project.

And if that's not a goer, then how about something a little more radical? We could pull down the Victoria Memorial outside the Palace and make a prime spot of real estate for The Goons' statue, or perhaps something even more grand: The Goons in the centre, and in the four corners we'd have the Pythons, Tony Hancock, Morecambe and Wise, and Alan Carr. Of course, I don't mean a statue of Alan Carr. I mean the real thing. Preferably shackled, with the nation's rotting fruit and veg surplus placed in baskets for the passing crowd.

I will leave it at that, hoping that the Goon idea excites you as much as it does me.

Ying tong yiddle I poing in your honour,

STAN MADELEY
THE UK'S TOP RICHARD MADELEY LOOKALIKE
BM NOUMENON, LONDON, WC1N 3XX EMAIL: STAN@STANMADELEY.COM

H.R.H. The Prince of Wales
Clarence House
St James's Palace
London, SW1 1BA

17th February, 2010

Sir,

I wrote you a letter last year regarding my idea of erecting a statue to Britain's comedy greats in Trafalgar Square. If you remember, I suggested that it should represent The Goons and I asked you to put your considerable shoulders behind the scheme given that my schedule is full due to touring commitments.

Since then, I have enjoyed a quiet Christmas, a somewhat merry New Year, a rather bleak January due to my wife, Sandra (54), undergoing an operation to remove minor shrapnel from her knee, and, thus far, a cold February in which my sinuses just haven't been right. What I have not enjoyed is any reply to my original letter despite my including an envelope and suitable postage to cover costs.

And speaking of costs, I have now invested three stamps, two sheets of quality Conqueror, and a few envelopes to this enterprise, and, I hasten to add, the 70 pence I already spend each year on my taxes to keep us going as a monarchical state.

Now, I'm not a man to begrudge the nation its pomp and circumstance – 70p is a mere drop in the sea, especially to a man like you who owns a sea or two, and I am happy to pay it. It's worth it for Brian Sewell alone, but to get the whole Royal Family for that price is an absolute bargain. However, I do expect certain standards such as common courtesy. Sandra (wife, see above) has been quite distressed by the thought of our letter ending up on some spike. I know that this was the way things were handled in centuries past, and I'm not saying that I would look quite handsome with my head on a pole, but surely you're not above a simple reply.

Whether you agree with my work as a lookalike, I merely wanted to see justice done for Spike, Peter, Michael, and Harry. They turned comedy around in this country and deserve an accolade more prominent than a blue plaque in Camden Town. Even Charlie Drake has one of those and I hardly consider 'My Boomerang Won't Come Back' as the zenith of British humour.

I will end by again stating my belief that a monarchy is the way to go. The French rejected the glory of the Sun King but accepted Jerry Lewis. That, in my opinion, says everything you need to say about the republican position. I will not, however, compound my mistake by including postage with this letter. You still have the stamp I sent you the first time and I would certainly like it back. It was blue and distinctly second-class, much like your humble correspondent.

Your friend in cabaret,

CLARENCE HOUSE
LONDON SW1A 1BA

From: The Office of TRH The Prince of Wales and The Duchess of Cornwall

Private and Confidential

9th March, 2010

Dear Mr. Madeley,

    The Prince of Wales has asked me to thank you for your further letter of 17th February, and was sorry to learn that you had not received the response to your previous correspondence.

    As you will see, I enclose herewith a copy of the letter which was sent to you on 18th November, and trust this one will now reach you.

    His Royal Highness has asked me to thank you once again for taking the trouble to write as you did, and to send his warmest best wishes to you and your wife, Sandra. The Prince trusts that she is recovering well from her knee operation, and that the problem you were having with your sinuses has now been resolved.

Yours sincerely,

Mrs. Claudia Holloway

Mr. Stanley Madeley

CLARENCE HOUSE
LONDON SW1A 1BA

From: The Office of TRH The Prince of Wales and The Duchess of Cornwall

Private and Confidential

18th November, 2009

Dear Mr. Madeley,

The Prince of Wales has asked me to thank you for your letter of 7th November in connection with your views on honouring some of this country's finest comedians.

His Royal Highness is grateful to you for taking the trouble to write to him as you did and for your suggestions, but regrets that he is unable to reply personally to your letter.

I am sorry to have to send you such a disappointing reply. Nevertheless, The Prince of Wales has asked me to send you his best wishes.

Yours sincerely,

Mrs. Claudia Holloway

Mr. Stanley Madeley

STAN MADELEY
THE UK'S TOP RICHARD MADELEY LOOKALIKE
BM NOUMENON, LONDON, WC1N 3XX EMAIL: STAN@STANMADELEY.COM

Sandy Alexander Robert Nairne 21st September, 2009
Director
National Portrait Gallery
St Martin's Place
London WC2H OHE

Dear Mr. Nairne,

Please allow me to introduce myself. My name is Stanley Madeley (by deed poll) and I am the UK's top Richard Madeley lookalike working in venues across London and the South East with my one-man surrealist show, 'Nude Mutton Trombones – The Stanley Madeley Experience Live!'.

With such an introduction, I don't suppose it comes as any surprise to you that I am writing with regard to the National Portrait Gallery's long-established refusal to include lookalikes in its collection. Of course, I understand the argument that a painting of Ken Dodd would look very similar to another painting of Harry Sprout, the nation's top Ken Dodd lookalike. However, haven't we progressed enough in our thinking to recognise that no one man should have the monopoly on bucked teeth, haywire hair and jokes about mother-in-laws?

I might argue that John Hurt doesn't look too dissimilar to Sir Ian McKellen. They are both established actors with distinguished careers behind them, but, let's face it: they both appear in the same sort of half-baked nonsense, whether that's *Hellboy 2* (Hurt) or *X-Men 3* (McKellen). And as much as I enjoyed Sir Ian's performances in *Lord of the Rings*, do you really need 14 portraits of the man, yet only have one of Anna Ford?

Do you see my point? If you can hang a picture of Richard Madeley on your walls, then why is there no room for the man who has spent the last 25 years entertaining audiences with his unique brand of musical saws, juggling, and experimental banjo? And can Richard play the bongos? Precisely! Yet you continue to adorn your walls with his (admittedly handsome) visage.

Here's what I propose: that you open a wing of your establishment to a gallery of lookalikes. It would be a parallel universe where noses are slightly askew, teeth more raised, jaws more prominent, or, in the case of Mrs. Shelly Dunne, the nation's No. 1 Anne Robinson lookalike, bears absolutely no resemblance at all since Ms. Robinson had her face remodelled after that of a dyspeptic Pekinese with bladder control issues.

If you don't mind my ending on such a personal observation: I have seen your own portrait and you strike me as a fair man with a look of merriment about his clear and undeniably striking eyes. Might this not be your chance to leave your mark on the National Portrait Gallery? I will await your reply with great anticipation, poised thusly: with one arm held aloft, the other on my knee beside the quilted drapes left casually to cover my loins.

Kindest regards,

[signature]

FROM THE DIRECTOR **Sandy Nairne**

National Portrait Gallery

Mr Stanley Madeley
The UK's Top Richard Madeley Lookalike
BM Noumenon
London
WC1N 3XX

8 October 2009

Dear Mr Madeley

Thank you for your letter dated 21 September regarding the inclusions of lookalikes in the National Portrait Gallery permanent collection.

As you may know from our original Charter, the National Portrait Gallery collects portraits of those who have made, and those who are making, a significant contribution to British history and culture. The National Portrait Gallery, London was founded in 1856 and houses the finest collection of portraits in the world. The Gallery aims to promote an appreciation and understanding of portraiture in all media, offering a unique insight into the lives of the men and women who have shaped British history and culture from the Middle Ages to the present day. With a varied exhibitions, displays and talks and events programme, and over 1,000 portraits on display across three floors - from Queen Elizabeth I and William Shakespeare to The Beatles and David Beckham - the National Portrait Gallery weaves together 500 years of history, art, biography and fame.

Alongside staging special exhibitions, the Gallery strives to display as much of the Collection as possible at any one time. We therefore operate a rotation system, alongside an extensive loans programme, in order to ensure that as many portraits as possible are exposed to the public view. Unfortunately, with over 11,000 paintings, sculptures and miniatures in the Gallery's Primary Collection alone - excluding the Photography Collection, and the Gallery's Archive Collections - the Gallery is unable to display the full Collection in the Gallery space at any one time as physical space is at a premium. Decisions about which portraits are suitable for inclusion in the Collection are made by the Gallery's team of expert curators, and approved by the Trustees.

I am afraid that your suggestion of a 'lookalikes' gallery is not feasible or appropriate.

I do hope you will be able to visit the Gallery again in the near future.

Yours sincerely

Sandy Nairne
Director

National Portrait Gallery St Martin's Place London WC2H 0HE
T 020 7306 0055 F 020 7306 0056 www.npg.org.uk

STAN MADELEY
THE UK'S TOP RICHARD MADELEY LOOKALIKE
BM NOUMENON, LONDON, WC1N 3XX   EMAIL: STAN@STANMADELEY.COM

Sir Terry Wogan
BBC Radio 2
99 Great Portland Street
London, W1A 4WW

5th October, 2009

My dear Sir Terry,

Please allow me to introduce myself. My name is Stanley Madeley (by deed poll) and I am the UK's top Richard Madeley lookalike as well as being a fifteen-year veteran of the London cabaret scene with my one-man show, 'Slingback Tan Daffodils – The Stanley Madeley Experience Live!'.

Sir, I must ask you to reconsider! I mean, of course, this nonsense I hear about your retirement. Both wife and self have been left mortified by the prospect of you abandoning us. Unless you plan to personally slide beneath our duvet in the morning (not, I should add, an unwelcome prospect) then this idea of handing your show over to Chris Evans is tantamount to asking Mr. Ozzy Osbourne to sing Nat King Cole. I'm sure there would be some who would enjoy it but there'd be others who'd rather perform delicate surgery on their own knees with the blunt end of a hysterical tomcat.

I suppose the BBC will expect me to continue to pay for my TV licence, but that's not likely to happen once you leave. World Wars have been fought over less and my dear wife, Sandra (54), has already enrolled at night school to learn suitable guerrilla tactics to fight this battle.

Based on previous examples of his work, it's clear that Mr. Evans doesn't have what it takes to fill your slot (if you'll excuse the phrase). How long before I wake up to the sound of a greased nanus live in the studio, playing parlour tricks with a block of lard and a fire extinguisher? How soon before Jonathan Ross is in your chair, talking about his bathroom habits?

There is, I feel, only one real alternative: I nominate myself as your successor. I have a charm that has been described as 'mellow', 'calming' and 'mildly off-putting' by people who have seen my cabaret act. I also enjoy singing along to obscure songs to which I provide my own lyrics. My version of the Beatles' 'Day in the Life' improves on the original in at least a dozen places. There's no talk of suicide or holes in Blackburn Lancashire in my version; just wholesome entertainment in the true spirit of the Wogan legacy.

Let me end this letter by thanking you for the very great pleasure you've given us over the years. Long may it continue, even if it does mean war. When you next see a 56-year-old mother of three chained to the top of Nelson's Column, you will know it is Sandra (54) by the flash of white thigh and the name Terence stitched onto the gusset of her thermal drawers. I'm sure that will change your mind, possibly about a great many things . . .

I remain, Sir, your humble servant,

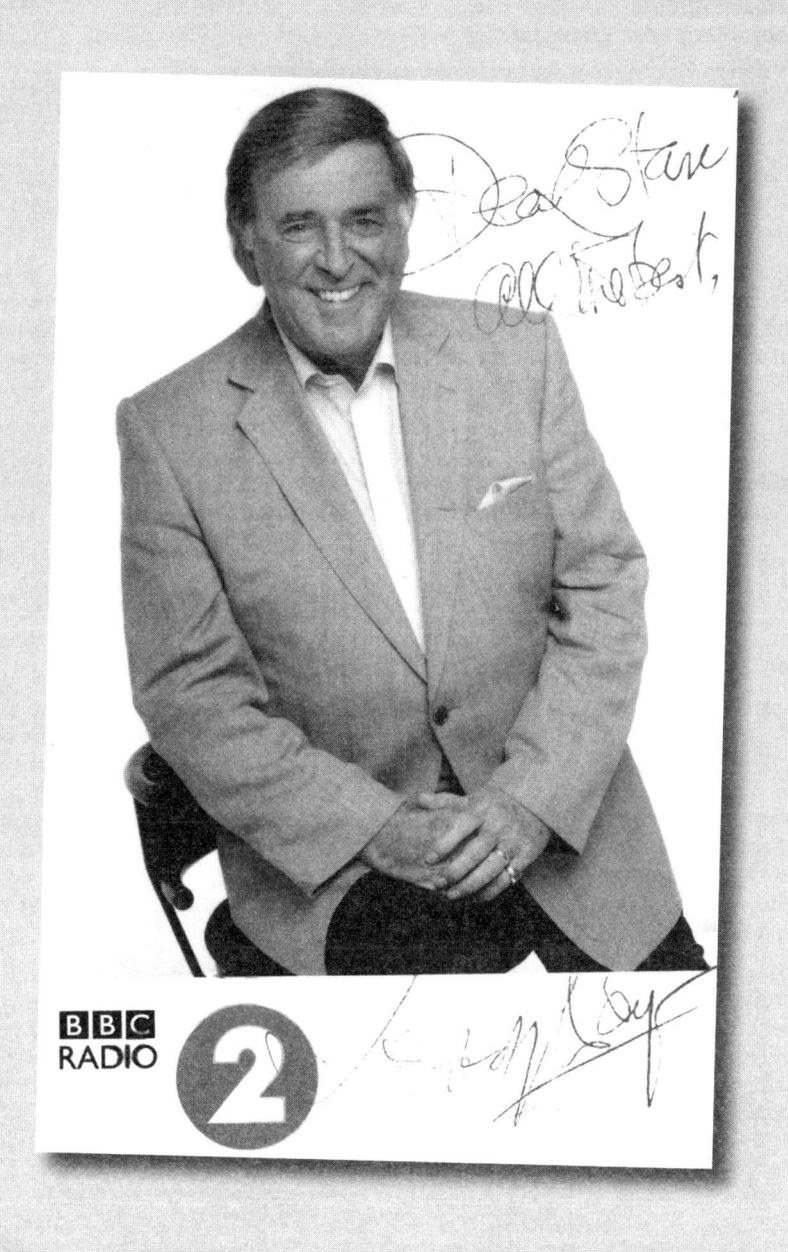
BBC
RADIO
2

STAN MADELEY
THE UK'S TOP RICHARD MADELEY LOOKALIKE
BM NOUMENON, LONDON, WC1N 3XX   EMAIL: STAN@STANMADELEY.COM

Mr. Manuel A. Noriega
Prisoner 38699-079
Federal Correctional Institution
Miami Fl 33177
United States

8th February, 2010

Dear Mr. Noriega,

Times are darkest just before the dawn. Or, as it appeared in your case: France!

It comes to something when a man in cabaret feels impelled to write to a man in prison but I've just heard the BBC news report that you might be sent to France. It's pretty shabby treatment, if you don't mind my saying, and I hope you fight this through the courts. How any judge can justify such treatment is beyond me.

But please ... Permit me to introduce myself. The name is Stanley Madeley (by deed poll) and I am the UK's top Richard Madeley lookalike and a seasoned veteran of the British cabaret circuit. Not that I suppose any of that means much to you but over here it means a lot.

You see, I'm an entertainer and, whilst I don't know a thing about politics, I do know an abuse of human rights when I see one. When you've done your time, you should walk away from prison a free man. Certainly, no man should be sent to France without a good reason. Didn't they say that even de Gaulle didn't want to go back?!

Listen, I'm very much a person who believes in keeping things upbeat and I thought you might appreciate a letter of support from a source, however unlikely. I know this is very much the business of the United States but not everybody over here in Europe believes everything they say. Certainly, not everybody on the North London cabaret circuit does. You have won many fans here in Luton because of the way you've conducted yourself in prison and it is with astonishment that we discovered that you're still being held in incarceration. They let out Jeffrey Archer without any fuss and I don't see any reason why they can't do the same for you.

I know this sounds a bit vulgar but is there any chance you could do my wife, Sandra (54), the very great honour of signing a photograph? I don't know if it will help but it might spread the news of your current problems to a wider audience whilst also providing inspiration to all who work in the nightclub. Needless to say: we are keeping our fingers crossed and we're all 'saying no to France'!

Your friend in cabaret,

Stan Madeley

No feeling of falling at 120 mph.
Photographed at the Lakewood Parachuting Center, Lakewood, N. J.
Tel. 201-363-4900.
Write for free brochure.

PARACHUTES INCORPORATED
Orange, Mass. Lakewood, N.J. Crawfordsville, Ind.

Sandra M.

Si Dios conmigo
Quién contra mi!!...
God is my shopper

Photo By: Lee Guilfoyle

M-30E

STAN MADELEY
THE UK'S TOP RICHARD MADELEY LOOKALIKE
BM NOUMENON, LONDON, WC1N 3XX   EMAIL: STAN@STANMADELEY.COM

The Rt Hon Michael Howard QC MP 25th January, 2010
House of Commons
London, SW1A 0AA

Dear Michael,

Chin up! These may be dark days but if the boy Gerrard can get back to his blistering ways, we'll once again be a mighty force in the Premiership! I've lost count of the number of times I've strained my groin and come back nimbler than ever. And what's not to like about playing a midfield of Mascherano and Lucas and pushing Aquilani into the hole behind a pacey striker?

But where are my manners? Allow me to introduce myself. The name is Stanley Madeley (by deed poll) and I earn 'top whack' as the UK's top Richard Madeley lookalike. I am also a star of the UK cabaret scene and, as you can tell, I'm a Liverpool fan too. And would you believe that I'm also married to a woman called Sandra (54)? Surely kismet is operating at its profoundest level on behalf of the two of us!

I am writing, you see, with some good news. I've just been booked to appear in a regular series of nightclub gigs in Liverpool. I'll be travelling up each week on a Saturday and a Wednesday, which, as you know, are days when El Niño often holds communion at Anfield. Naturally, given that you're a big Liverpool fan, I thought you might be heading there yourself. I wondered if you fancied a lift.

Before you start commenting to your own lovely wife Sandra that some crackpot has written to you with the most outrageous offer, let me say that it's a lack of creative thinking that has cost this country so dear in the past few years. You've been in the House of Commons longer than dry rot but I bet I'm the first person to ever write to you to suggest that you join in the car pooling revolution. Yet why should that be? It would cut down on emissions and we could split the petrol bill 50/50. Or if you don't fancy 50/50, I'll go as far as 70/30 to make it easier on the parliamentary ombudsman. I'm always good for a few rum anecdotes and my driving style has been described as 'arrogant', 'haphazard' and 'negligent' by the AA, no less. There's never a dull moment with me behind the wheel, Michael!

I would only ask that you sit up front. I don't like people sitting behind me when I'm driving and, to be perfectly honest, I like to keep the back seat free for the cage containing my two trained stoats, 'Dennis' and 'Skinner', who form an important part of my act and private life.

Look, now I've made the offer, could I not persuade you to stay around a little longer? You've always been my favourite Tory. As a proud wearer of the blue rosette, I believe in a Burkean conservatism predicated on a free and tolerant society where history is our example and nature our model. That said: Michael Gove just gives me the willies.

Your friend in the Citroën Aura J Reg,

From: THE RT. HON. MICHAEL HOWARD, Q.C., M.P.

HOUSE OF COMMONS
LONDON SW1A 0AA

Stan Madeley Esq
B M Noumenon
London WC1N 3XX

Our Ref: MH/LP

4th February 2010

Dear Mr Madeley

Thank you for your letter of 25 January and your very generous offer of transport up to Liverpool on a Saturday or Wednesday. I very much appreciate the thought behind it and, if opportunity presents itself, may well take advantage of your generosity.

I do note, however, that you make no reference to a lift back!

Your definition of Burkean conservatism can hardly be bettered.

With best wishes

MICHAEL HOWARD

STAN MADELEY
THE UK'S TOP RICHARD MADELEY LOOKALIKE
BM NOUMENON, LONDON, WC1N 3XX   EMAIL: STAN@STANMADELEY.COM

The British Trombone Society   7th September, 2009

~~[redacted]~~

~~[redacted]~~

Hail, Fellow Trombonists!

Allow me to introduce myself. My name is Stanley Madeley (by deed poll) and, as perhaps you are aware, I am the UK's top Richard Madeley lookalike and a well-known cabaret act with my touring show, 'Tungsten Tipped Windmills – The Stanley Madeley Experience Live'. What most people don't know is that I'm also a semi-professional trombonist, having been introduced to the instrument by the great Bernie Clifton in 1974.

For that reason, I am sitting here eager to despatch my application form so that I might join your extraordinary society. However, I am also plagued by great indecision. Why so? Well, as much as I dearly want to join your society, I've had a rival offer to join 'The British Flute Society'! I was wondering if you could match or better their current bid.

For a yearly fee of £45, The British Flute Society are offering me: four quarterly editions of *Pan* (the journal of The British Flute Society); reduced rate entrance to many British Flute Society events; discounts on instrument insurance for my flute; access to a variety of flute-friendly venues across the UK, as well as a chance to quiz their panel of expert flautists about all matter of flute-related business at the flute seminars held each year at their flute jamboree. I will also receive a membership badge (flute-shaped), a membership card (laminated with my picture in colour – they've asked for a photo of me holding a flute), as well as a handy shoulder bag with the catchy tag 'I blow flute ...' printed on the side in tasteful italic lettering.

Naturally, my heart is with you and your Trombone Society but I'm extremely aware of getting the most 'bang for my buck', so to speak, and the Flute Society offer does appear very attractive. Sandra (wife, 54) insists that we must save for a new conservatory and I'm not one to disagree with her or the men at Safestyle UK. It means I have to be cautious with my money. However, my heart is set on pursuing leisure opportunities in a trombone-rich environment.

I will wait a little while before making my decision in the hope that you trombonists can come through for me. Many of my best friends are trombonists and some of the most memorable moments of my life have revolved around that fine instrument.

I hope you can find your way to making your offer more appealing (perhaps a trombone-shaped badge and some personalised mute/hat for my trombone) and I eagerly await your reply.

Sincerely yours,

[signature]

Stanley Madeley (Trombonist)

To: stan@stanmadeley.com
From: Geoff Wolmark
Date: 23/09/2010 21:44
Subject: BTS Membership

Dear Stan, thank you very much for your letter regarding membership of the British Trombone Society. There are several categories of member, if you follow this link you will see them:

http://www.britishtrombonesociety.org/membership/bts-membership.html

As a member you will get three copies of the Trombonist magazine a year, free admission to most BTS events, access to our web-based members' forum and the warm glow from knowing you are part of the Society for players of the king of instruments.

If you were prepared to perform at one of our BTS events, we would offer you a year's free membership, but you would have to become a member in order to get a free year. We do not pay anyone to play, to avoid any charges of favouritism, but we do offer travel expenses.

Why not come to one of our events and see for yourself what we get up to, bring your trombone and have a great day with others of the same ilk.

The next BTS day is on Sunday, 4th October at Oundle School. Full details on the news page of our web site, click here:

http://www.britishtrombonesociety.org/news/latest-news/index.html

Hope this is helpful and look forward to meeting you.
With best wishes
Geoff Wolmark
BTS Secretary

```
S   T   A   N         M   A   D   E   L   E   Y
THE  UK'S  TOP  RICHARD  MADELEY  LOOKALIKE
BM NOUMENON, LONDON, WC1N 3XX   EMAIL: STAN@STANMADELEY.COM
```

The British Flute Society   7th September, 2009

Dear Flautists,

Allow me to introduce myself. My name is Stanley Madeley (by deed poll) and, as perhaps you are aware, I am the UK's top Richard Madeley lookalike and something of a permanent fixture on the British cabaret circuit with my surrealist stage act, 'Electric Midget Boogaloo – The Stanley Madeley Experience Live'. However, what you might not know is that I am also a virtuoso on the flute!

This being said, you find me in a state of high anxiety with the membership forms for your excellent society spread out across the dining room table. All the forms are filled (black biro), the cheque is written (Barclays) and I have attached a label (Avery) to the envelope. However, I am hesitating before I post them because I have had some news, this morning, which casts a new light on my application. I have just received a rival bid from The British Trombone Society!

Naturally, if I had the money, I would join both of your societies. Being a highly musical man, I love both instruments passionately. If I had to choose, I suppose I would say that I prefer the flute. However, The British Trombone Society has put together a very generous membership package. My dear wife, Sandra (54), is a somewhat miserly woman, though loving too. She only gives me enough allowance each month to join one of your organisations. I was wondering if you could 'up' your offer, and make it more attractive to a man on limited budget and requiring more 'bang for his buck', if you see what I mean.

Currently, The British Trombone Society is offering me: complimentary copies of their *Club Trombone* magazine; discounted trombone books, merchandise and paraphernalia; a place on their yearly 'Trombone March' around Ashby-de-la-Zouch in the East Midlands; a membership pin (shaped like a trombone), along with a membership card (fully laminated) and a choice of rucksack or 'bum bag' emblazoned with the logo of the British Trombone Society and the pleasing bon mot 'Love my bone!'

Clearly, it's a generous package and I'd be a fool not to consider it seriously. However, as I said, my heart lies with the flute and my fellow flautists. With only a few add-ons (perhaps some kind of lapel badge and free carry case) you could easily convince me to join your society.

I hope you see my predicament and can do something to ease my indecision. I sincerely thank you for your time and I look forward to your reply with great eagerness.

Best wishes,

Stanley Madeley (Flautist)

Mr Stanley Madeley
BM Noumenon
LONDON
WC1N 3XX

The British Flute Society

11 September 2009

Dear Mr Madeley,

I regret that British Flute Society cannot offer such delights as an annual trot around a strangely-named British town, or an instrument-shaped piece of jewellery, or a laminated membership card (I fear ours are but simple pieces of stout paper), or indeed any piece of logo-emblazoned personal luggage, and we certainly can't match the poetry of the British Trombone Society's 'Love my bone'. I am therefore at a loss to think of something the British Flute Society can do to entice you to join us beyond telling you that we publish a journal that is the envy of instrumental societies around the world, that we mount a biennial four-day event at which the world's finest flute players perform for us, that we are mounting a series of Master Concerts at music colleges around the country and that the world's best and most intelligent flute players are members of our society.

You see, Mr. Madeley, we do not require baubles and gimmicks to attract members who, like you, are intelligent and perceptive. Surely, sir, the offer of a few tacky gewgaws would not sway a man of your stature?

Yours sincerely

J. N Rayworth

John Rayworth
Membership Secretary

STAN MADELEY
THE UK'S TOP RICHARD MADELEY LOOKALIKE
BM NOUMENON, LONDON, WC1N 3XX EMAIL: STAN@STANMADELEY.COM

John Rayworth
The British Flute Society

21st October, 2009

Re. Bloody Trombonists

Dear John,

Many thanks for your reply to my letter of the 7th September. I'm sure that you'll be impressed to learn that despite the current post strike, it still only took four weeks to get here. I also trust that you remember me. My name is Stan Madeley (by deed poll) and I'm in cabaret.

If you recall, I'm also into flutes in a big way but have recently been seduced by the trombone. That prompted me to write to you regarding bribes/incentives and you replied with a compelling argument for my joining The British Flute Society. And, to be perfectly frank with you, John, your reply was superior in every way to the response from those bloody trombonists. I don't know what you think about them but I'm sure there must be something unhappy in the lives of trombonists to make them such a dull lot. I suspect it's the fact that 40% of their instrument is behind them. It must put them on edge, living with the fear that 40% of interesting things are happening out of sight. I hesitate to call them paranoid but one is tempted to believe that they're just that. In fact, I won't hesitate to say it at all: all trombonists are paranoid. And you have my permission to use that on a BFS t-shirt.

Anyway, I'm writing to convey the good news that I've decided to join The British Flute Society immediately. You seem a thoroughly decent bunch of individuals, which is more than I can say of British trombonists. You'll be impressed to learn that I have now bought myself a flute and I've enjoyed the first of my free flute lessons with Mrs Spruce, who only lives up the road. I've also bought myself a bowler hat, satin waistcoat, and, as you can see, I've grown a goatee since last I wrote.

Can I just say, John, that this is the life! My dear wife, Sandra (54), sits with me each night and accompanies me on her drums as I play along to the collected hits of Acker Bilk. I still haven't got the fingering quite right and I can't move the end of my flute in seductive patterns like he does, but I'm getting there and I'm sure my application to join your august body will encourage me further.

Could you send the relevant documents so I can get my application lodged with the right people? And before I close this letter, can I ask: do you do discounts on reeds? I seem to be going through one a week at the moment, which I understand is typical of a beginner. I can't stop chewing on them! Mrs. Spruce keeps calling me a 'biter', which led to some confusion in this household, I can tell you!

Best wishes,

Stanley Madeley (Flautist)

Mr. Stanley Madeley
BM Noumenon
LONDON
WC1N 3XX

29 October 2009

Dear Mr Madeley,

Thank you for your interest in The British Flute Society. I have enclosed an application form for you to complete. Unfortunately as the flute is a none reed playing instrument we are unable to offer discounts on those goods. Indeed it worries me a little that your flute teacher Mrs Spruce calls you a "biter" when you are playing an instrument which does not have a reed attached. I note however that your photograph shows you holding a clarinet which does indeed have a reed.

Please return the form to me:

John Rayworth
Membership Secretary
The British Flute Society

Yours sincerely

J N Rayworth

John Rayworth
Membership Secretary

Registered Charity No. 326473

STAN MADELEY
THE UK'S TOP RICHARD MADELEY LOOKALIKE
BM NOUMENON, LONDON, WC1N 3XX   EMAIL: STAN@STANMADELEY.COM

Joint Commission on Biochemical Nomenclature   15th September, 2009
Department of Chemistry
Queen Mary University of London
Mile End Road
London, E1 4NS

Dear Sirs/Madams/Drs/Professors/Underpaid Research Assistants,

Allow me to introduce myself. My name is Stanley Madeley (by deed poll) and, as you can see, I pride myself on my uncanny resemblance to Richard Madeley, the TV chat show host. But please don't let that fool you! Though I tour the UK with my one-man surrealist show, 'Kentucky Hopscotch Monster – The Stanley Madeley Experience Live', during the day, I work in the field of organic chemistry and it is with regard to my day job that I write to you.

I have noted that in many chemistry publications (*Chemical Science*, *Chemical Week*, *What Chemical*) the sugar-ring oxygen atom has been designated by the nomenclature O1'. However, recently, I have realised, with some confusion, that the sugar-ring oxygen atom is now being designated O4'! Would it be too much to ask for a little consistency in our chemical nomenclature? After all, we're not Bulgarian and there are some people to whom chemical nomenclature means a lot. Personally, I feel unbalanced when these changes happen without reasonable warning. Think on, ladies and gentlemen, think on!

On a second point, do you happen to know if there's an association I might join which would allow me to pursue my interest in chemical nomenclature during my leisure time and long weekends? Indeed, might I be so bold as to nominate myself as a member of your commission? I'd be happy to take the work on an unpaid basis, have impeccable manners and a zeal for the subject that's almost a mania. I often find myself waxing lyrical about chemical nomenclature and there's nothing that gives me more pleasure than discussing chemical nomenclature with my family and friends. To that end, I've written you a sonnet (attached) and I wonder if you could do me the very great honour of reading it out at the next meeting of the Joint Commission on Biochemical Nomenclature.

Thank you for giving me a little of your valuable time and I wish you well in the exciting and rapidly changing world of nomenclature (biochemical). I suppose you get letters like this all the time but let me end by being the first to say that if you're ever in the mood for some cabaret with a biochemical nomenclature twist, you now have my contact details. Tickets will be waiting for you at the door.

    Kind regards,

    Dr. Stanley Madeley, Ph.D.

A Sonnet to the Joint Commission on Biochemical Nomenclature Inspired By the Nomenclature of Junctions and Branchpoints in Nucleic Acids

by Stanley Madeley

Oh, you foolish folded nucleic acids,
Of which branchpoints are a feature,
Dost thou double-stranded DNA
Generate sequence rearrangement?
Or do you bewitch, being calm and placid,
And by secondary and tertiary folding
Of single-stranded nucleic acid
Still make this a happy-ever-ending?
Yet, branchpoints in a DNA molecule
Are welcome homes to friendly enzyme,
Who, being free to roam, hip and cool,
Will bind at DNA junctions given time.
The complexity of junctions never slows!
The need for new nomenclature always grows!

International Union of Pure and Applied Chemistry
Division VIII Chemical Nomenclature and Structure Representation
Joint Commission on Biochemical Nomenclature

School of Biological and Chemical Sciences
Queen Mary University of London
Mile End Road, London E1 4NS

30 September 2009

Dr S Madeley
BN Noumenon
London WC1N 3XX

Dear Dr Madeley

Thank you for your letter of 15 September. The recommended designation of the ring oxygen of cyclic forms of aldoses is not O1 because it is ambiguous. There are two oxygens at this position. In the furanose ring form the designation as O4 is unambiguous and also indicates the ring size. More commonly of course it will be C5 with the pyranose form. O1 is then available to indicate the oxygen which is not in the ring. This numbering was agreed by experts in the field from around the world and was then presented for public review in 1981 before the recommendation was finally approved. It is unfortunate if some publications do not observe this recommendation. Regrettably we have no powers to insist on its use.

I guess the organisation in Britain which is most concerned with chemical nomenclature is the Chemical Structure Association. You might also consider the Chemical Information and Computer Applications Group of the Royal Society of Chemistry. I am assuming you are a member of RSC. Another approach is to watch the IUPAC web site where new recommendations are posted at the stage where they available for public review. Any comments are welcome. After the review process the document will be revised, if necessary, before approval as IUPAC recommendations.

Yours sincerely

Dr Gerry Moss
President Division VIII

STAN MADELEY
THE UK'S TOP RICHARD MADELEY LOOKALIKE
BM NOUMENON, LONDON, WC1N 3XX   EMAIL: STAN@STANMADELEY.COM

Mr. Stuart McCullough
Sales & Marketing
Bentley Motors Limited
Pyms Lane
Cheshire, CW1 3PL

8th October, 2009

Dear Sir,

Allow me to introduce myself. My name in Stan Madeley (by deed poll) and I am the UK's most successful Richard Madeley lookalike currently working in cabaret. As you might know, I'm coming up to my sixtieth birthday and, as a treat to myself, I have been preparing to buy a Continental GT from one of your dealers down here in London. From my many test drives, it is clear to me that the GT is an extraordinarily fine automobile. You should be extremely proud of it.

As you can perhaps imagine, I've also spent these months visiting your showrooms with my wife and deciding on the colour of my new car. I thought I had it settled when I declared to Sandra (54) that I'd chosen Venusian grey. However, it has now come to my attention that the footballer, Mr. Stephen Ireland (Manchester City), has bought one of these cars for his girlfriend. Naturally, his choice of Bentley is a convertible (a GTC, I believe), with a stunning red roof which provides a striking (pun intended) contrast to the predominately white body, which itself has red trim, red hubcaps, and numerous air vents. The interior is predominately red but with large swathes of white leather fashioned to perfection. He has also had the words 'To Jess With Love From Stephen' stitched (within a heart) into the headrest of the driver's seat.

I would like to just thank all your staff for the work they put into persuading me to buy a Bentley.

I will now be buying a Jaguar.

Your most humble servant,

[signature]

No reply!

Take themselves a bit seriously, don't they, love?

STAN MADELEY
THE UK'S TOP RICHARD MADELEY LOOKALIKE
BM NOUMENON, LONDON, WC1N 3XX   EMAIL: STAN@STANMADELEY.COM

CITIBASE Manchester
40 Princess Street
Manchester, M1 6DE

22nd September, 2009

Re. Stanley's Gibbons (North)

Dear Sir/Madam,

Allow me to introduce myself. My name is Stanley Madeley (by deed poll) and I am the UK's top Richard Madeley lookalike working across London and the South West with my one-man show, 'Chronic Cheese Slaughter – The Stanley Madeley Experience Live!'.

Having established long-standing connections with the lookalike community in the south, I have recently opened my own talent agency (ironically titled, 'Stanley's Gibbons') providing celebrity lookalikes for all manner of publication and production. The business has become extremely successful and I am now looking to do the same in the north.

Could you send me pricings for your largest office, ideally with space for both an administration suite and a small photographic studio? We would also require certain assurances that we can remain discreet about our work given that many of our lookalikes are stars in their own field. Some, such as Ms. Felicity Grope, the nation's top 'Annette Crosbie' lookalike, have won awards in the world of high-class hardcore pornography where the craze for lookalikes is currently at a peak. Most, however, are stars of the routine cabaret circuit. Indeed, they make up the majority of our business and I would anticipate that there would be relatively little graphic nudity involved in our Manchester operation.

With regards to your offer: do you provide telephone and Internet access? If so, what are your wireless networking options? I am looking to trial some Internet services involving lookalikes – an opportunity to 'surf a star' – and, depending on the scheme's popularity, I intend to expand it in the near future.

Finally, we would require access to a bathroom and a kitchen. Is your facility serviced by a company that can deliver clean drinking-water to the office daily? We would also require fresh fruit with plenty of extra-large sized bananas.

I'm sure that our troupe would bring value to your current location. I'm often told how staff in our London offices are cheered up by the sight of Fred Zimmer, the nation's top Bruce Forsyth lookalike, doing his funny little trot up the corridors, or the sound of Ruby Prune, the nation's top Cilla Black lookalike and vocal artiste, singing to them as they work. Perhaps you could give us an entertainers' discount for making your lives more enjoyable. But listen to me! I'm sure life at Manchester's Citibase is little short of fun all the time! I bet there's not an unhappy bone in that whole wonderful complex of luxury office space!

I look forward to your reply and eagerly anticipate what I'm sure will be very competitive rates.

Cheers,

Stanley Madeley (President and Impresario)
Stanley's Gibbons

Mr. Stanley Madeley Esq.
'Stanley's Gibbons'
BM Noumenon
London
WC1N 3XX

30th September 2009

Dear Stanley,

Thank you so much for your recent letter regarding office space with Citibase Manchester, it was both informative and entertaining! The lookalike business sounds most eventful – and certainly more risqué than I ever imagined!

The cost of an office here with Citibase Manchester would really depend on what you are looking for – we have many different sized offices and prices vary accordingly. The best way to price the space would be to advise of an all-inclusive, fully serviced cost of approximately £150.00+VAT per workstation. Essentially it would all depend on the number of staff you would need the space for. The cost of a photographic studio would, again, depend on the amount of space required.

The cost quoted includes business rates, utilities, cleaning, reception services and broadband. The broadband provided would be your own 8MB line, and the monthly rental is included in the price quoted. Broadband is subject to a one-off install charge of £150.00+VAT.

We would be happy to offer any further services required, such as the fruit baskets you mention, but may not be able to guarantee the 'extra large bananas' you have requested. Manchester's climate is unfortunately not famed for it's fruit-growing successes!

As you have so rightly guessed Citibase Manchester offers a fast-paced and fun-filled environment – you must be psychic! (An extraordinary talent, bearing in mind you have already been blessed with your remarkable similarity to Richard Madeley!) Your agency couldn't help but add to the charming mix of clients here – and you are right – we would undoubtedly be cheered up by Fred Zimmer, the nation's top Bruce Forsythe lookalike, 'doing his funny little trot up the corridors'.

Whilst we would be delighted if you chose Citibase for your new enterprise, we would have to draw the line at any 'graphic nudity', as you describe it, on the premises. Our company phrase may be 'Freedom At Work' but we have to draw the line somewhere! Aside from this we can assure you of our discretion at all times.

I would suggest the best way of discovering whether Citibase would be the right choice for you would be to visit us and have a look at the space – we'd be happy to show you around and discuss you needs further.

Please do not hesitate to contact me if you require any further information.

Kindest regards,

Rhianon Murray
Citibase Manchester

Cc. Mr. Thomas Cotterill

STAN MADELEY
THE UK'S TOP RICHARD MADELEY LOOKALIKE
BM NOUMENON, LONDON, WC1N 3XX EMAIL: STAN@STANMADELEY.COM

Evan Davis
Today Programme
BBC Radio 4
Room G630, Stage 6
Television Centre, Wood Lane,
London, W12 7RJ

4th September, 2009

Dear Evan (if I may),

Allow me to introduce myself. My name is Stan Madeley (by deed poll) and I am the UK's top Richard Madeley impersonator and a fully licensed speech therapist working out of offices in London.

Having been a long-time listener to Radio 4, I was somewhat dubious when you took over the *Today* show. I wasn't sure if a man possessing a typical 'Dorking drawl', as we professional speech therapists call it, would have the right gravitas to host such an important programme. I should never have doubted you! It is an absolute delight to have your voice wake me up each morning. What a rich tone you possess, less than a semi-tone above middle C.

However, whilst you are due much praise, it would be remiss of me not to provide you with a professional assessment of your pronunciation. I must simply ask you to **consider your vowels**! I believe you elide your long 'e's beyond that required for a man of your slender girth and considerable height. A shorter 'e' would improve the quality of broadcast immeasurably. You should listen to how John Humphrys did it. You can't find a better schwa (ə) in the business and, as for his fricatives, his palatal technique is second to none.

I believe in you, Evan, and for this reason, I have developed a series of exercises that can help both your enunciation and your posture. They can easily be done in the confines of a studio; lift your arms, carefully clench and unclench your buttocks and repeat the following mantras:

- 'Extended elbow exercise ensured Evan enjoyed enhanced enunciation.'
- 'Every error evaded Edward, elevating Eliza's enjoyable epidural.'
- 'Exterior eaves entombed eleven expired ermine, engorged earlier, earning ennobled Earls excessive economic enhancement, especially expensive earmuffs!'

If you'd be interested, I'd be happy to send you the rest of the lessons free of charge. In the meantime, you should prepare by buying yourself a pair of loose fitting crushed velvet slacks with good ventilation, a rubber ball (non-solid), and some cloves of garlic. We'll have you fixed in no time!

Best wishes,

Room G630 BBC Television Centre
Wood Lane London W12 7RJ

19 November 2009

Dear Mr Madeley

Thank you for your very entertaining letter of 4th September. Please accept my apologies for only now just getting round to replying to it.

I will attempt your suggested exercises when I get a chance to. Maybe you will be able to spot the difference!

With best wishes

pp Evan Davis

Stan Madeley
B M Noumenon
London
WC1N 3XX

STAN MADELEY
THE UK'S TOP RICHARD MADELEY LOOKALIKE
BM NOUMENON, LONDON, WC1N 3XX   EMAIL: STAN@STANMADELEY.COM

Mr. John Perkins
Managing Director
Specsavers Optical Group
St Andrews
Guernsey, GY6 8YP

22nd September, 2009

Dear Mr. Perkins,

Please allow me to introduce myself. My name is Stanley Madeley (by deed poll) and I am the UK's top Richard Madeley lookalike, currently appearing across the country in my one-man surrealist show, 'The Norway Protection League – Stanley Madeley Unleashed!'.

You should have gone to Specsavers! You should have gone to Specsavers! You should have gone to Specsavers! You should have gone to Specsavers! You should have gone to Specsavers!!!

I could continue but I'm sure you grew tired of that pretty quickly; in fact, almost as quickly as my own antipathy to this mantra has developed over the last couple of years. No sooner do I walk on stage and start my knife-throwing act than some wise guy in the audience will loudly question my choice of spectacles. I needn't add that this is extremely dangerous and my good wife, Sandra (54), has received many fleshy nicks because of it. Yet the abuse doesn't stop there. Rarely does a moment pass when I'm out shopping when I don't hear somebody mutter or cry: 'He should have gone to Specsavers!'

Yet the irony in all of this is that I *did* go to Specsavers. My current glasses were chosen for me by a member of your staff who fluttered her long lashes at me and told me in a breathy voice that I looked simply adorable and ever so handsome.

I know this is probably going to fall onto deaf ears but is there any chance that you might change your slogan to something that won't be used to victimise the myopic? Would you have come up with a similar slogan if you were in the business of selling prosthetic limbs? I hardly think so. Imagine a world in which yobs could abuse the disabled with cries of 'He should have gone to Stumpsavers!' You see my point? It may have started as a novelty but it has become a hindrance to the widespread social acceptance of men, women and children who wear spectacles.

I hope you give this letter proper attention but somehow fear that you won't take me seriously because of my glasses. Indeed, for that reason, I will not express my disappointment that you have also destroyed an icon of childhood by putting Postman Pat in designer specs. I will simply end by saying that I have worn glasses for all my adult life. Despite my criticisms, I don't believe there has been a company that sells such a range of high quality and stylish frames. Certainly, I believe none have done such an excellent job of complimenting my own unique and award-winning features.

Sincerely yours,

Specsavers

La Villiaze
St Andrews
Guernsey
Channel Islands
GY6 8YP

Tel: 01481 236000
Fax: 01481 235555

Specsavers Online:
www.specsavers.com

Mr Stan Madeley
BM Noumenon
LONDON
WC1N 3XX

October 9 2009

Dear Mr Madeley

Thank you for your letter, addressed to John Perkins, of September 22. I was certainly troubled to read of the rather cruel audience reactions you've experienced, particularly as you say that your glasses were actually from us.

I can only put this down to one of two reasons. First, that on seeing you in your splendid glasses, certain members of your audience become overcome with jealously and misguidedly try to score cheap points off you by mis-using our phrase. Or second, everyone *thinks* they can do comedy... I can't think of any other reason because the member of the store team who chose your glasses would have been specially trained to ensure they suited you. Quite frankly this game - rather like yours I imagine - is all about keeping our customers happy so that they remain loyal; hence it's just not in our interest to sell you glasses that don't look good. (By the way I had a look on your website and noted that your forthcoming shows were selling out extremely quickly, so it appears you're well capable of satisfying your customers).

I do appreciate though, that these unhelpful comments can affect your concentration at key parts of your performance and I hope your wife's flesh wounds have healed.

I also take your point about our phrase becoming used rather cruelly. That's a bit of a curate's egg for us because we're obviously happy that it's become so widely accepted and adopted, but a little disappointed that it's not always used intelligently or applied with consideration for the person at whom it's aimed. It's linked to my earlier opinion that at times people simply use it rather lazily to try and get a cheap laugh. My guess is that the people who care about you would never dream of making these remarks. Within our advertising we certainly make it very clear that the unfortunate party either needs a sight test, or is wearing glasses that are so obviously awful that there is a stark reason why they should visit us. I'm afraid though that on balance the phrase is so successful for us I can't see us changing it in the near future.

However perhaps there is a solution. I'd hate to think you were too nervous to wear your glasses in public - and why shouldn't you - but if you haven't already, may I suggest you investigate contact lenses for these occasions? You were kind enough to compliment our choice of glasses and I can tell you with some pride that our range of contact lenses is equally fine and very reasonably priced. I think if you were to return to the Specsavers store you bought your glasses from, that same lady will tell you in a similarly breathy voice how good contact lenses can be. Might that also put a stop to your slightly wayward knife-throwing too?

I hope you do feel that I've addressed your concerns sufficiently. I need to correct one small point you've raised though and that is that we haven't put Postman Pat (who's probably on strike somewhere right now) in designer glasses - we just showed him breaking his current glasses...which of course allows us to use our line.

Hope the tour goes well.

Yours sincerely

Tim Orton
Director of Marketing & Planning

INVESTOR IN PEOPLE

Registered Company
Specsavers Optical Group Limited
Registered in Guernsey
No. 12294
Registered Office
La Villiaze, St Andrews,
Guernsey. GY6 8YP
Directors
A List of Directors is available
from the Registered Office

03/09

STAN MADELEY
THE UK'S TOP RICHARD MADELEY LOOKALIKE
BM NOUMENON, LONDON, WC1N 3XX   EMAIL: STAN@STANMADELEY.COM

Mr. Tim Orton
Director of Marketing & Planning
Specsavers Optical Group
Guernsey, GY6 8YP

21st October, 2009

Dearest Tim,

Thank you for your letter of the 9th October, replying to mine of the 22nd September. I hope you remember me. My name is Stan Madeley and I'm in cabaret.

'Thinks'

The italicising of this word has caused much debate in the Madeley dinette in recent mornings. My dear wife Sandra (54) believes that you meant nothing by it. I, on the other hand, believe it barbed. You've read *The East Hackney Chronicle*, haven't you? You were deliberately quoting Mr. Barlow who wrote: 'Stan Madeley is personable but unfortunately thinks he can do comedy'. Well, if this is a battle of wits, sir, let me quote the email I've just received from Su Pollard's assistant: 'Thanks for your letter to Su. I'm afraid that due to her extremely busy schedule she won't be able to take part. All the best with your show.'

I think that answers you!

I must add, however, that your slight was fairly compensated by the excellent suggestion you made elsewhere in your letter. As you can see, I took your advice and had contact lenses installed in both sockets. The world is suddenly sharper, my field of vision improved, my attractiveness to ladies possibly trebled. My wife even said that she finally saw the man she married all those years ago. Unfortunately, I was in Specsavers at the time, so I missed him.

Disappointed, naturally, that you refuse to change your long-standing and highly successful catchphrase on my say-so. I've been preparing to provide you with equally catchy bon mots:

- Specsavers: it's the vision thing
- Specsavers: we're next door to Boots!
- Specsavers don't poke you in the eye like they do at Visionexpress
- At Specsavers, we can not only provide stylish glasses that will improve your vision, we can also diagnose serious underlying medical conditions!
- Pet spectacles now at Specsavers

I've only worked on these for a few weeks so imagine what I'd come up with if I dug deeper.

My wife's flesh wounds are healed well, thank you for asking, though Sandra's recent ear loss had taken her mind off them.

Can I end by thanking you again for such an excellent reply? I wish everybody were so generous and embracing of our shared humanity in a way that demonstrates that we are not the mere cogs of industry, but individuals who like to laugh, smile, sing, and throw knives.

Accordingly, you deserve my very best wishes,

STAN MADELEY
THE UK'S TOP RICHARD MADELEY LOOKALIKE
BM NOUMENON, LONDON, WC1N 3XX   EMAIL: STAN@STANMADELEY.COM

Elton John
████████████
████████████

17th September, 2009

Dear Mr. John, or if you'll permit me to be 'familiar', Elton,

Allow me to introduce myself. My name is Stan Madeley (by deed poll) and I am the UK's top Richard Madeley lookalike and a star of the London cabaret scene.

I am writing to you in a state of disbelief after learning that your plans to adopt have fallen through due to official interference. Sadly, bureaucrats understand nothing of life. I, however, pride myself on not being a bureaucrat and I believe I have a solution. As luck would have it, I find myself in the very unique position to make an adoption happen for you. Not only would I be an absolutely first-class son but the papers could be signed within a week. I could even have my lawyers draw them up.

Naturally, in such an unusual situation (dare I say groundbreaking?), you would think that the usual questions of cuteness would have to be put to one side. But that isn't so. I'm astonishingly cute, as you can see from the enclosed colour glossy (signed). I might add that they are available in wallet size and would look absolutely stunning on top of a white baby grand.

I have been fully vaccinated and have already passed all my exams up to post-graduate degree level with flying colours. So, from Day 1, you can tell people how proud you are of me and how I take after you in terms of good looks and inordinate bundles of talent. What's more, with me you'd be certain that there'd be none of the usual trouble that accompanies teenagers. I won't be turning up on your doorstep at half past three in the morning with a drunk young girl called Mildred who happens to be tattooed on the neck with the insignia of the British Nationalist Party. In fact, I'm much more likely to go for a good night in front of the TV. Who knows: we might even enjoy the same programmes! Do you like *Time Team* and *Top Gear*? I also make an excellent curry, which is more than you can say about any of Madonna's nippers.

Can I offer you anything more? Only the certainty that I'd follow you into showbiz. You know, Dad, I've received some rave reviews for my surrealist one-man show, 'Happy Baboon Liposuction – The Stanley Madeley Experience Live'. It would fill you with floods of joy to hear me sing 'Honky Cat' on my Casio.

So, there you have it. It's the full adoption package but without the usual problems. I've changed my name once and I'd be happy – nay delighted! – to change it again.

Look at this face, Elton? How can you say 'no' to eyes such as these?

Your loving son,

[signature]

[handwritten note:] What do you mean? He must have replied... He wouldn't orphan me... Not Elton... Not now... Papa!!!!

STAN MADELEY
THE UK'S TOP RICHARD MADELEY LOOKALIKE
BM NOUMENON, LONDON, WC1N 3XX   EMAIL: STAN@STANMADELEY.COM

The Mother General
Tyburn Convent
8 Hyde Park Place
London, W2 2LJ

30th September, 2009

Dear Sir/Madam,

Allow me to introduce myself. My name is Stanley Madeley (by deed poll) and I am the UK's top Richard Madeley lookalike. You probably haven't seen my long-running show, 'Glory Egg Revolution – The Stanley Madeley Experience Live!' and I can't say that you've been missing much! It may have been hugely popular among students and those within London's techno/acid-trance culture, but I have found it deeply unfulfilling as both artist and man.

I am writing to you, then, in a state of profound dissatisfaction with my life. Just because I drive a Bentley (a Continental GT, no less!) and wear expensively tailored suits, it doesn't mean that I'm happy. To me, the world lacks meaning. It is too obsessed by material wealth and there is no longer any sense of that fruitful 'something' that makes it all worthwhile. My life is missing its spiritual cement.

After having spent the whole morning in silent contemplation, I now believe that I'd like to cast aside my dressing gown (silk) and take up the robes of your order. I want to leave behind all the commuting, profit hunting, taxation, nuisance phone calls, vandalism, noisy neighbours, mole infestations, rugby tackles, Norwegians, DVD piracy, hecklers, congestion charges, Swine Flu, body piercings and ornamental rockeries. I want to come and join your convent; on a part-time basis, to begin with, but I'm sure that once you see what a meaningful contribution I can make, you'll be only too happy to make it a permanent booking.

I understand if you have your reservations. You wouldn't have risen to the rank of Mother General, probably clearing fifty grand a year or more, without having a keen eye for troublemakers. I don't fully understand what it is that you do at Tyburn Convent or what's required from me before I join. But I do have a feeling that I'm cut out for something more meaningful than crooning on the cabaret circuit. I seek the solitude of devoting myself to something bigger than Blackpool's summer season.

I hope you don't think it strange that a man so successful and, dare I say, handsome, should seek this kind of change in his life. If you would permit me to join your convent, I could perhaps use some of my skills in the convent's cause. About 80 per cent of my act is family friendly and, should there be any other members of the convent who are musical, we could easily form a small barbershop quartet and sing close harmony for the poor and needy.

Thank you for your time. I'm sure that, within Tyburn Convent, I will find the all-inclusive society of like-minded men and women that I so desperately crave. Naturally, I eagerly await your response.

Bless you,

Stan Madeley

**Adorers of the Sacred Heart
of Jesus of Montmartre** OSB

THE MOTHER GENERAL, TYBURN CONVENT, 8 HYDE PARK PLACE, LONDON W2 2LJ. ENGLAND 020 7723 7262

10th October 2009

Mr Stanley Madeley
BM Noumenon
Lndon WC1N 3XX

Dear Stanley,

Thank you for your letter dated 30th September 2009. Tyburn Convent is exclusive for women, however I have enclosed some information on Benedictine male orders for you to equire about the Benedictine life. Be assured of our prayers for your needs and intentions.

In ther Sacred Heart
Yours sincerely

Mother Hildegarde
Secretary General
PP Mother General

123

STAN MADELEY
THE UK'S TOP RICHARD MADELEY LOOKALIKE
BM NOUMENON, LONDON, WC1N 3XX EMAIL: STAN@STANMADELEY.COM

Sir James Dyson
Dyson Ltd
Tetbury Hill
Wiltshire, SN16 0RP

7th October, 2009

Dear Sir James, or, if you'll allow me to 'innovate', Jim,

Permit me to introduce myself. My name in Stan Madeley (by deed poll) and, as you might know, I'm the award-winning Richard Madeley lookalike working out of London. You might even have seen my show when it was in your neck of the woods back in April.

Being a man who likes to own the very latest in vacuum technology, I was naturally the first in the queue to buy your cleaner based around a ball. As soon as I saw you talking about it on TV, I thought to myself: 'Jim Dyson's got balls! What a genius he is!' Soon after, wife and self were hugely excited to welcome a new member of the family; a DC25 Animal (£332.76, free delivery). However, we have experienced some technical problems and I felt morally bound to write to you.

Mrs. (Sandra, 54, 5' 2") does all the cleaning as per her job spec (housewife). She usually begins near the TV and works her way across the room and into the adjoining dining area where the dog (Perry Como, 3, 2' 4") spends most of his day licking what you probably imagine dogs lick. The first day the vacuum arrived, my wife decided to give it a spin. I was a bit busy with the Sudoku so I merely observed from the sidelines. She vacuumed around the sofa (commenting to the point of tedium about how easy it was to turn) before pausing a moment to pick up the dog's toys which Perry Como had left lying next to our aquarium. I wasn't paying much attention or at least, not until I heard a squeal of delight followed by the less pleasurable sound of Sandra's head impacting against tropical fish tank.

From what I understand, my wife had turned around and bent over to pick up the toys. Then, suddenly and without warning, she'd received the hefty handle end of the vacuum in her sensitive rear inch. How had that happened? After much investigation, it was discovered that our living room has a five-degree list. Naturally, we have been shocked by the news; almost as shocked as my wife when receiving the full force of your cleaner mid and centre.

This, I feel, demonstrates a design flaw of your otherwise quality vacuum; I mean, what kind of man would secure a heavy-duty suction device onto something as unstable as a ball?

Now, I'm sure they don't give all those awards to men who are in the business of goosing women, so what I'm writing to ask, Jim, is what you're going to do about it? I will simply finish by thanking you for your time and for many years of pleasure spent with your other excellent suction devices.

Sincerely yours,

Mr Stan Madeley
BM Noumenon
London
WC1N 3XX

15th October 2009
Ref: AG/GEN/1-3J6E5F

Dear Mr Madeley,

Thank you for your letter to Sir James dated 7th October 2009. Due to the huge amount of mail he receives, Sir James cannot reply to all letters personally, so he has asked me to respond on his behalf.

I am very sorry to hear of the circumstances that have led to you contacting us, and hope that your good lady has made a full recovery following the incident.

When in the upright position, the DC25 sits not only on the ball but also the stabiliser at the back, and the cleaner head at the front. If the cleaner is not fully locked in the upright position there is always going to be the potential for the machine to automatically engage the brush bar which lowers the wand handle. If your cleaner had been correctly locked into the upright position this unfortunate accident would not have taken place.

In view of the above I can confirm that there are no inherent design issues with the DC25 vacuum cleaner.

Our customers' comments and feedback are always appreciated whether complimentary or critical and we do have a feedback system.

If you require any further advice or assistance please do not hesitate to contact our customer Helpline on telephone number 0800 298 0298 between the hours of 7am to 10pm, seven days a week.

Yours sincerely

Andy Greenman
Customer Liaison

DYSON LIMITED
TETBURY HILL
MALMESBURY
WILTSHIRE
ENGLAND
SN16 0RP

TEL 01666 827200
FAX 01666 827299
HELPLINE TEL 0800 298 0298
FAX 08706 060039

www.dyson.co.uk

STAN MADELEY
THE UK'S TOP RICHARD MADELEY LOOKALIKE
BM NOUMENON, LONDON, WC1N 3XX   EMAIL: STAN@STANMADELEY.COM

The League of Cruel Sports
New Sparling House
Holloway Hill, Surrey

26th September, 2009

Dear Sir/Madam,

Allow me to introduce myself. My name is Stanley Madeley (by deed poll) and I am Britain's top Richard Madeley lookalike and the progenitor, director and star of 'Sherbet Fizz Waltz – The Stanley Madeley Experience Live!' I am also an experienced leisure promoter with a particular passion for expanding the market in extreme field sports within the UK.

On a recent tour of the Huesca region of Northern Spain, I came across a wonderfully archaic peasant sport, which has long since died out in England. I have researched the market and I believe it would be highly profitable should we reintroduce it to the country over the course of the next year. To that end, and given your expertise in the field of cruel sports, I wondered if I might seek your advice.

The sport is basically a version of the old English sport of 'weasel curling' but with a few rules that make it authentically Spanish. Whereas the English variant used linen bags packed with dried peas – forming the 'weasel', as in the old nursery rhyme 'pop goes the weasel' – the Spanish game uses a real weasel, bred for its ability to withstand impact as well as its aerodynamic qualities. As I am sure you'll appreciate, the use of live animals makes it much more exciting for the spectator, though I suppose there might be a concomitant response from the animal welfare lobby for which we might have to prepare! We could begin to offer the sport in invitation-only locations around the country, so we could establish it without official interference. As you might know, the weasel is still considered a nuisance in the UK and I'm sure we'd have the support of farmers whose land we could clear of these particularly vicious creatures.

As to the rules: there are two teams of five people, each with their own 'throwing weasel', known in Spanish as *el buzón*. One player from each team takes a turn to throw (*surtidor*) their weasel by its tail (*el carrito*). After five rounds (three throws each), the furthest throw (measured from the second bounce) is the winner. However, if the weasel lands on its feet, the throw is considered invalid (*sacapuntas*) and the weasel is put down with the judge's 'grimping' mallet (known in Spain as *el codo* and very popular with the locals who celebrate by eating a weasel paella).

I think with the right organisation behind it, the sport has a natural home in the UK. Of course, we would have to arrange transport to move our boogle (the technical term for a collection of weasels) around the country but I think this is the least of our problems. Given your long established history of organising cruel sports, I hope you can provide some helpful feedback.

Sincerely yours,

Stan Madeley

Stanley Madeley, President
Uncle Stanley's Amazing Animal Circus

13th October 2009

Mr Stan Madeley
President
Uncle Stanley's Amazing Animal Circus
BM NOUMENON
London
WC1N 3XX

New Sparling House
Holloway Hill
Godalming
Surrey GU7 1QZ
Tel: 01483 524 250
www.league.org.uk
mail@league.org.uk

Dear Mr Madeley

Weasel Curling

Thank you for your letter of 26th September.

I fear you may have misunderstood our organisation as we are the League **Against** Cruel Sports, not the League **of** Cruel Sports. Consequently I am sure you will appreciate that we would be very concerned to see weasel curling introduced as a sport in this country.

We do have a proposition to make to you, however, which would bring together your excellent skills as the UK's top Richard Madeley lookalike – and having seen your photograph we are impressed – and your quest for new and interesting sports.

The League believes that a suitable, popular and welfare friendly substitute for the cruel sport of weasel curling, would be green wellie hurling. This sport requires a combination of dexterity, skill, balance, and the ability to select the best green wellie from those available for hurling.

The basic rules would be that the wellie must land within the target, known as the pit; the foot of the wellie must on landing be at exactly ninety degrees to the thrower and the leg of the wellie must be exactly in line with the thrower. Deviations in the leg line of the landed wellie in the pit to the left are know as 'Brown degrees' and degrees to the right are known as 'Cameron degrees'. Degrees of difference to the right angle either to the left or the right of the foot of the wellie are known as 'Cleggs'. A wellie landed outside the pit is known as a Lembit and a wellie that lands on its feet in the pit which remains standing, is known as a League and is a winning wellie, trumping all other wellie scores.

Scores for degrees off line are summed and if no wellie is left standing, the green wellie showing the least deviation in score points known as cruel degrees is declared the winner.

It is a rule of the hurling that all hurlers must accept the rule of law and that no animals or people shall be hit harmed or endangered by the hurler. All wellies to be hurled must previously been used in the countryside in work and any wellie found to have been used or worn in town shall be automatically disqualified from the hurling competition.

The order of hurling shall be determined by height, with the shortest hurler hurling first and the tallest last. For the avoidance of doubt, hight is determined by adding the girth and height measurements of the would be hurler, who must be wearing the wellies he or she plans to hurl in competition.

We would be delighted to discuss this with you in more detail should you wish.

Yours in wellies,

Douglas Batchelor
Chief Executive

Registered Charity No. 1095234   Registered in England & Wales as a Company No. 04037610   Registered Office: New Sparling House, Holloway Hill, Godalming, Surrey GU7 1QZ
Printed on recycled paper

STAN MADELEY
THE UK'S TOP RICHARD MADELEY LOOKALIKE
BM NOUMENON, LONDON, WC1N 3XX EMAIL: STAN@STANMADELEY.COM

Douglas Batchelor
Chief Executive
The League *Against* Cruel Sports
Holloway Hill, Surrey
GU7 1QZ

18th November, 2009

Dear Douglas,

Many thanks for the letter of the 13th October and apologies for the delay in answering. My wife and I have been down in Africa hunting big g... I mean ... lounging with Germans by the pool.

Thank you for clearing up the slight confusion regarding your organisation. I must thank you too for the suggestions regarding rule changes in the sport of weasel curling. I can see the very many advantages to be had by using Wellington boots instead of the traditional weasel, not least the better grip that a rubberised boot gives the thrower. In wet weather, a weasel's tail can become very slippery and tends occasionally to come off in the hand. I admired enormously the nuances regarding leg displacement, though fear that the natural bias of the media would see most throws as being classed as 'Brown degrees'.

However, this is all academic. To tell you the truth, Douglas, I have had a change of heart about the whole weasel curling business.

Your letter touched me in a way that I would never have thought possible. During our recent holiday in Africa, there came a moment when I was lying next to the pool watching my friend Hans take a drink of water. At that moment, your words came back to me and I realised that killing creatures for sport is utterly futile, if not morally outrageous.

As Hans lowered his snout into the water, I found myself lowering my gun and turning to my wife with a tear in my eye.

'I can't do it, Sandra,' I said. 'What has this poor creature ever done to us to make us want to hurt it?'

My wife, who was of course also lying by the pool, lowered her gun too and smiled.

'You know, Stanley,' she said, 'I've never really been much of a fan of lying by the pool.' Or words to that effect.

But the point is, we turned around and walked back to the Land Rover vowing that we would never hurt another creature again.

Unfortunately, at this point, Hans charged us and gored my wife cruelly. I fired off a couple of wayward shots and the noise scared Hans away back into the cocktail lounge before I managed to drag Sandra to the Land Rover. But, you see, Douglas: animals (or Germans) deserve to be left alone. You are clearly doing good work and I wish you well as you tirelessly strive to soften the hearts of the men and women who hunt deer, bait badgers, fight dogs, harry chickens and force ferrets to play hopscotch.

You have changed me, Douglas! Wellington boots it shall be!

Sincerely yours,

STAN MADELEY
THE UK'S TOP RICHARD MADELEY LOOKALIKE
BM NOUMENON, LONDON, WC1N 3XX   EMAIL: STAN@STANMADELEY.COM

Michael White
The Guardian
90 York Way
London, N1 9GU

28th October, 2009

Re.: Balls

Dear Michael,

Cracking diaries! Keep them up!

But, please, allow me to introduce myself. The name is Stanley Madeley (by deed poll) and I'm the UK's top Richard Madeley lookalike, currently slaving away at the coal face of British cabaret with my one-man show, 'Westminster Knee Jerk – The Stanley Madeley Experience Live!'.

Now, I know you hold a candle for Gorgon Brown but to write that Ed Balls suffers from a 'slight charm deficit' ('Barry's Balls "bully" beef', 19th October) is an act of such staggering understatement that you had me feeling sorry for the man. He's not worked hard to become the government's chief child catcher only for you to offer him affection. You need to look yourself in the eye in your shaving mirror each morning and repeat: 'I come to bury Balls, not to praise him.' You need to be more TUC and much less TLC.

I wonder if you're experiencing a crisis of confidence, a bit like my wife's dog, Clarkson, who suffered a dislocated jaw last year after trying to chew a coconut. You both seem afraid to bite Balls. Yet, Michael, your snap is one of the best in the business. I always sit up in my seat when you appear on Sky News. Of course, it's a pretty lousy news channel at all other times, primarily since they've started to repeat themselves every fifteen minutes like some addled Lear in a home for retired thespians. But wife and self look out for you when we can. Sandra (wife, 54) will often say, 'Oh, turn it back! Michael White's coming on in a bit ...' Two hours later, you'll finally appear and the waiting will feel like it was worth it. Sandra usually then suggests that I should grow a moustache like yours. She says it makes you look distinguished.

My point is, Michael, that such a distinguished tash should stop arguing such tosh. Give us more meat and less offal and ground beak. I enjoyed your radio show, *Savaged by a Dead Sheep*, and I encourage you to do more savaging of your own.

Let me end by mentioning that I'll be running one of my self-improvement seminars in the New Year, based around my knife-throwing act. If you fancy rebuilding your confidence by throwing blades, drop me a line.

A 'slight charm deficit', indeed!

Your friend in cabaret,

Stan Madeley

To: stan@stanmadeley.com
From: Michael White
Date: 27/11/2009 16:56
Subject:

Hi there,

you were kind enough to write last month, offering to help boost my confidence and allow me to stand up to Ed Balls.

thanks for the offer, but I think I'll be ok without it.

I have kept your stamped addressed envelope.

Thanks for that too. Every little helps.

best wishes

To: Michael White
From: stan@stanmadeley.com
Date: 27/11/2009 19:09:10
Subject:

Dear Michael (if I might be so bold and I believe I might since you've already walleted my stamp),

First of all, thanks for the cracking email!

Secondly, what's a first rate chap like you doing keeping second class postage? I didn't get that from Quentin Letts at the Mail. He sent me a signed letter that included the word 'corker'.

Thirdly, point taken re confidence.

Fourthly, damn the environment: I've just printed out your reply ten dozen times and I'll be handing them around tonight's meeting of the Michael White Glee Club (Luton branch).

Fifthly, my wife has just gasped 'such a lovely man' and I am not about to disagree. To receive a reply from you yet Prince Philip still can't be bothered!

Sixthly, don't vote Rantzen!

Seventhly (and lastly), keep up the good work! With a bit of luck and perseverance, I'm sure the Daily Mail will spot your extremely enviable talents. The important thing is to keep trying!

Your friend in cabaret,

Stan

To: stan@stanmadeley.com
From: Michael White
Date: 28/11/2009 18:20
Subject:

Dear Stan,

thanks for the latest note and news.

It now seems I have your second class stamp - I always use second class stamps, it's a cheaper stamp than the first class and the service is no worse - and you have my email to share with the Glee club.

It seems a fair swop, 20p worth of wit and wisdom. If I'd known you were planning to publish it I would have tried a little harder.

If you are in contact with Quentin do remember that he is even more nimble than you seem to be at publishing other people's private emails, remarks, contents of bins etc. Does very well at it.

You have been warned.

Best wishes

To: Michael White
From: stan@stanmadeley.com
Date: 28/11/2009 19:19:11
Subject:

Dear Michael,

You catch me in thong, about to go on stage, so I have to be brief (pun intended).

Delighted with your improved offer but to suggest that it's 20p for second class mail dates your last visit to a Post Office to the December of 1983. Second class is now 30p and not a penny less. That said: you will undersell yourself! You provided far more than twenty pence worth of wit. There was at least five pence more.

Your words also struck me as typical of a Rantzen supporter. Quentin understood where I stood on that score and gave me his veiled support.

The Michael White Glee Club went well, thank for you asking. Motions were passed in your favour. The password for the month is 'Bercow'. As for the cheap bin remark (which I thought very much below you): cabaret, like Korean cuisine, is a man-eat-dog business. So is writing for those of us in the gutter of obscurity, selflessly bringing joy into the lives of strangers whilst also paying for the postage.

However, I note the warnings of the gulag at the bottom of your email and will abandon my book at 140,000 words of sparkling wit. You're right and I apologise. I'm doomed to dance for a living.
On which note, it's time to oil up and bring joy into the lives of some middle-aged secretaries on a hen night.

I remain, despite your censure, your earnest friend in cabaret,

Stan

STAN MADELEY
THE UK'S TOP RICHARD MADELEY LOOKALIKE
BM NOUMENON, LONDON, WC1N 3XX   EMAIL: STAN@STANMADELEY.COM

Polar Regions Unit   3rd December, 2009
Overseas Territories Directorate
Foreign and Commonwealth Office
London, SW1A 2AH

Dear Sir,

Having studied the Foreign Office website in great detail for over an hour, I now believe that you are the men (and, indeed, women – mustn't forget the fairer sex!) I must contact in order to receive a permit to undertake an Antarctic adventure.

Allow me to introduce myself. The name is Stanley Madeley (by deed poll) and I'm the UK's top Richard Madeley lookalike, as well as being a veteran of the extreme cabaret circuit. You might have heard about our recent exploits on the news; we were the first performers to stage a variety show on the top of Scafell Pike, Cumbria. It was a hugely successful event, raising nearly £300 for charity – only marred by the accident to Mr. Betteridge, our stilt walker, who fell over some scree and severely twisted his right timber.

The success of our recent stunts has now made me even more determined to become the first man to juggle his way to the South Pole. I will not be alone on this expedition. My dear wife, Sandra (54), will be accompanying me to record the trek on camera (Sanyo) and to control our huskies and sled. Sandra's mother will provide support from her sheltered accommodation in Salford. We anticipate that we would be on the ice for no more than two months, though we will have to be somewhat flexible since it all depends on how many times I have to pick up my balls.

I expect that you will greet this idea with some incredulity. Yet my track record is second to none in the field of extreme cabaret. I have recently juggled my way from Swansea to Cardiff and back again. And if you doubt my ability to handle the extreme temperatures, I would point you to my longest trek, from Edinburgh to John O'Groats, which took place on a particularly chilly week last November. I have also juggled for 48 hours without a break for this year's Children In Need, raising £418.33 in the process and receiving a signed photograph of Sir Terry Wogan (a copy of which I enclose – you may keep it, I have plenty) as a thank you.

I would be very grateful if you could send me the relevant documents and details about transport to the Antarctic. Any help that HM's government could give me would naturally be extremely welcome, though I wouldn't like to put you to too much trouble. A ship with a rescue helicopter in case of an emergency would be all that I would ask.

In the true spirit of adventure and following in the tradition of Scott, Fiennes, and Noakes,

I remain, your humble servant and explorer,

Stanley Twisleton Madeley

To: stan@stanmadeley.com
From: Lesley Peto
Date: 11/12/2009 11:38
Subject: Reply to letter of 3rd December regarding planned Antarctic visit

Dear Stan,

Many thanks for your letter dated 3rd December regarding your aim to be the 1st person to juggle your way to the South Pole.

Our permitting process is detailed on our website, the link is as follows;

http://www.fco.gov.uk/en/travel-and-living-abroad/your-trip/antarctica-visitors/permits-for-expeditions/

The Antarctic Act 1994 notes all expeditions to Antarctica must be fully self sufficient. We are therefore unable to offer any assistance to you during your planned trip. We will also be unable to provide a rescue helicopter or any other help, advice or assistance in this regard. It is the sole responsibility for the permit applicant to demonstrate to us that they have the necessary coverage before they are granted a permit to enter Antarctica. You will therefore need to demonstrate to us you have;

- Search and Rescue coverage in case of emergency;
- Contingency plans covering every eventuality/emergency;
- An adequate risk assessment;
- Insurance coverage applicable to Antarctica;
- The necessary experience you have to conduct this activity in Antarctica, including necessary Antarctic experience.

As you can see from the link the process is very detailed and also very expensive. The majority of our applicants plan an expedition to Antarctica years in advance of the planned trip, ensuring they resource the necessary experience from Antarctic logistics operators, you are therefore being very optimistic to note you aim to complete this activity in the Spring of 2010. I will also conclude by noting that all expeditions to Antarctica must fit into one or more of the following priority areas;

- Education and Outreach
- Heritage
- Environmental protection and minimising Human Impacts;
- Science.

Yours Sincerely,

Lesley

Polar Regions Unit
Overseas Territories Directorate
Foreign and Commonwealth Office
WH 2.308, King Charles Street
LONDON
SW1A 2AH

S T A N   M A D E L E Y
THE UK'S TOP RICHARD MADELEY LOOKALIKE
BM NOUMENON, LONDON, WC1N 3XX   EMAIL: STAN@STANMADELEY.COM

Mr. John Timpson
Timpson Ltd
Claverton Road
Manchester, M23 9TT

7th December, 2009

Dear John,

A spot of sharp braking yesterday caused my wife to headbutt my glove box, when out should drop your book, *How to Ride a Giraffe*, which I've been reading at the traffic lights for some months now. I just hope you won't mind the extra media attention my own recent business success might bring your way.

But please, allow me to introduce myself. The name is Stanley Madeley (by deed poll) and I made my money in the lookalike business. With my uncanny resemblance to Richard Madeley (chat show host, raconteur, pundit and wit), I have become a seasoned veteran of the corporate cabaret circuit over the past fifteen years. I've recently put my capital into a new venture, which has become a blazing success. Wife and self have just opened our very first cobbling stall in a local shopping centre. Following the example you set out in your magnificent *Cobbled Together*, I have taken a very 'hands-on' approach with my staff. Delighted to say: it's already paying dividends! I occasionally drop in on the booth and offer encouragement as Sandra (54) grafts away at people's heels. There has been some worker unrest, but I think it's a small price to pay for business success. I'm sure you know what it's like spending a night or two in the spare bedroom because of a labour dispute!

Anyway, I'm contemplating purchasing another cracking read from your website. The volume titled *Some Facts About Timpson* has caught my eye but the description is somewhat brief: 'A small but perfectly formed book with facts about Timpson and our services and our unique way of doing things!'

I am very much an advocate of your 'way of doing things', John, but £3.99 (plus an additional 98p for post and packaging) seems a lot to pay for such a slim read. Can you give me any assurances that it's worth almost £5 and is there a facility to purchase a signed copy? And do you do autographed photos of yourself, preferably whilst cobbling?

Might I also ask if you have any other books in your pipes? I was thinking you could hit the hardback charts with a suitable volume on crime and punishment. I read your column in *The Telegraph* this week (enjoyed it, as always) and I was particularly inspired by the final line: 'Every thief gets the sack!!!' (exclamation marks mine). Terrific stuff, John! Every businessman must handle the grubby end of the boot. If we can't send our workers/wives down for a stretch at HM's pleasure, we can at least turf them out on their dirty lugs should they dip into the till.

Your friend in cabaret and cobbling rival,

Stan Madeley

From JOHN TIMPSON CBE
CLAVERTON ROAD · WYTHENSHAWE · MANCHESTER · M23 9TT

14th December 2009

Dear Mr Madeley

Thank you for your amusing and thought provoking letter. Please let me know where your shop is located so I can call in sometime and sympathise with your long-suffering wife.

You ask my advice – which I am happy to give – 'Some Fact about Timpson' is poor value at £3.99, simply because it is out of date. Your letter has prompted me to take it off sale prior to producing a more up to date account of the Timpson business.

Better to hang on to your cash and wait for further books which are in the pipeline.

Yours sincerely

John Timpson

John Timpson

Stan Madeley Esq
B M Noumenon
London
WC1N 3XX

STAN MADELEY
THE UK'S TOP RICHARD MADELEY LOOKALIKE
BM NOUMENON, LONDON, WC1N 3XX   EMAIL: STAN@STANMADELEY.COM

Mr. John Timpson
Timpson Ltd
Claverton Road
Manchester, M23 9TT

24th December, 2009

Dear John,

How delightful it was to receive your letter in the morning post. And on Christmas Eve, no less, so you catch me slightly merry on the mulled wine! Please excuse my typing if it occasionally strays into the function keys.

Thank you also for your kind words about our new business startup but, on that score, there's bad news, I'm afraid. Our key-cutting/chisel-grinding/cobbling outlet failed last week and we were forced to vacate our premises in the local shopping centre. To be perfectly honest, John, it all turned rather unpleasant as my wife, Sandra (54), wasn't for being evicted quietly. She even threatened security staff with a handful of Yale blanks, which, as you will know, carry a rather cruel edge to them when in the wrong hands.

However, evict her they did and Sandra (54) now sits moping at home, though the seasonal recourse to rum punch has helped cheer her a little in recent days. The good news is that I expect her mood to improve considerably tomorrow morning. I have put a few more coins in your pocket and made Sandra a Christmas gift of a pewter tankard with a glass base bought from your Warrington branch. It will be just the thing for her to drink her homemade mead.

Regarding my business, I intend to re-evaluate my position in the New Year, hopefully with advice gleaned from your books. As you can see, John, I'm a man very much about getting on his bike, peddling hard and making things happen.

It's just a shame that the current retailing environment is such a steep slope. The traditional services are being edged into the unprofitable parts of town. Nobody wants to have boots cobbled. They simply go out and buy new when the old could have been repaired with a cheap rubber sole. The nation cries ecology but wastes natural resources more than ever. I sometimes wonder if people think that rubber grows on trees!

As it is, I am saddened to learn that my previous letter has resulted in the withdrawal of your book. Examining the website this morning, I noticed that *Some Facts About Timpson* is no longer available. As I mentioned in my previous letter, I am very much an advocate of your 'way of doing things', John, and £3.99 (plus an additional 98p for post and packaging) now seems such a paltry amount for what was sure to be an engaging read.

However, it's not my job to question your business knowhow. If you feel you should recall the volume, then recall it you must! However, I have now made your shop my homepage and I will be checking daily to see if you've got something new on the shelf.

Let me end by wishing you well for the New Year and hope that you have another excellent twelve months of cobbling.

Your friend in cabaret,

STAN MADELEY
THE UK'S TOP RICHARD MADELEY LOOKALIKE
BM NOUMENON, LONDON, WC1N 3XX   EMAIL: STAN@STANMADELEY.COM

Mr. Terry Gilliam
███████████
███████████
███████████
███████████

7th December, 2009

Dear Terry,

Forgive this letter so close to Christmas – have a 'Merry One', by the way – but I had an epiphany last night re the title of your next feature film, *The Man Who Killed Don Quixote*. But please, where are my manners? Allow me to introduce myself. The name is Stanley Madeley (by deed poll) and I'm the UK's top Richard Madeley lookalike, as well as one of the country's top cabaret acts, currently appearing in the alternate beanstalk panto, 'Jacqueline's Knee Stalker – The Stanley Madeley Experience Live!'.

Quality showbiz is my territory, Terry, so when I heard that you plan to have another stab at Cervantes, I slapped my head and whistled through my bridge. It's the cardinal rule of cabaret that you give the punters what they want and I have to ask you: what is *The Man Who Killed Don Quixote* to your average Joe Q. Toothache? Having worked cabaret audiences for some fifteen years, I can tell you what works and what doesn't and you certainly won't bag the Jeffrey and Mary Popcorns of this world with a title like that. They wouldn't know Quixote from a shredded oat. However, I believe I can help you and add that 1 per cent of magic that will transform your project from 'interesting addition to the canon of cinema's leading auteur' to 'surprise box office sensation that became the most popular ride at Disneyland with a line of donkey-based action figurines'.

Why not change it to 'The Man Who Killed Don Quixote's Puffin'? Immediately, it puts Brenda Shopping-Trolley in familiar territory. It's The Lion King. It's Babe. It's Skippy the Bush Kangaroo. This might mean a few rewrites but I think it's worth it if we get some Oscar nods. In fact, I relish a good rewrite! Consider the scene, early in Act I: we're in a shack on the plains of La Mancha. Quixote is with his new (English/American) squire, newly returned from gathering food for breakfast.

Don Quixote: What's that on the end of yon lance, my young squire?

Squire Arnold of Altringham/Albuquerque: Ah, 'tis the guillemot I plucked from the air this morn.

Quixote: A guillemot? That's no guillemot. The plumage is all wrong.

Arnold: No, no, it's definitely a guillemot, my Don. I definitely heard it squawk when my lance lacerated its rearward facing vent.

Quixote: Vent? Vent? Spare me tales of the vent before breakfast ... And why, Arnold, do you attempt to hide yon bird by thrusting thy pole through yonder window?

A scuffle ensues in which Quixote snatches the lance from his squire's hands. Arnold makes his escape on the back of a mule as the Don falls to his knees, the dead bird in his lap.

STAN MADELEY
THE UK'S TOP RICHARD MADELEY LOOKALIKE
BM NOUMENON, LONDON, WC1N 3XX   EMAIL: STAN@STANMADELEY.COM

> **Quixote** (solus): Oh, Barry! Barry! What has happened to you, my dear sweet innocent puffin? Damn that man. I'll hunt you down, Arnold! I'll hunt you like the puffin murdering scoundrel that you are!

Etc. etc. etc. all the way up to 550 million quid in box office receipts and a seat for one on Keira Knightley's lap.

I know you're very much a visual man so I've enclosed a quick 'storyboard' of the opening scene.

Can I end by saying that it's the highlight of my long and frankly insignificant life to be part of this exciting project? Merry Christmas again! I enclose SAE for my working copy of your current draft.

Your thumb on the nation's pulse,

The Man Who Killed Don Quixote's Puffin

Sorry to say that my
Script is still classified
information —
    Seasons greetings

What a curt fellow!
No wonder this film is
still not made when he
rejects serious offers.
And not a mention
of my puffin idea!

STAN MADELEY
THE UK'S TOP RICHARD MADELEY LOOKALIKE
BM NOUMENON, LONDON, WC1N 3XX   EMAIL: STAN@STANMADELEY.COM

John Bannister
Managing Director
Warrington Borough Transport Limited
Warrington, WA4 6PT

5th October, 2009

Dear Mr. Bannister,

Please allow me to introduce myself. My name is Stanley Madeley (by deed poll) and I am the UK's top Richard Madeley lookalike, currently travelling the country with my one-man show, 'Gnnrrr Fllllrrr Paarp – The Stanley Madeley Experience Live!'.

You might wonder why I'm writing, so let me give you a clue! I'm an experienced driver with a deep and abiding love of speed. There's nothing that gives me more pleasure in life than accelerating hard followed by a prolonged spell of heavy braking. If I have passengers in the car, I like to see them alternatively pinned to their seats and then thrown forward accompanied by the agonising sound of their seatbelts snapping along with their necks.

The reason I'm writing is that I always thought I'd be happy with my career in cabaret but a recent visit to Warrington convinced me that I should aspire for more. I want to drive a bus in a wilfully negligent manner; causing elderly passengers who have yet to find their seat to go sprinting down the aisle like Usain Bolt after a sub-eight-second world record. If they could then run face first into a metal pole, that would make me even happier. Then I'd throw the bus around a corner, causing my other passengers severe discomfort. I don't know about you, sir, but I'm only happy if I've managed to detach the retinas of strangers by hitting them with a huge load of horizontal G-force.

I also pride myself on my indifference and would love the opportunity to go sailing past a bus stop crowded with passengers when it's raining, adopt a gruff unpleasant manner towards people when they have the affront to board my bus, or to snap at people with mobility issues because they're not boarding the bus as quickly as they should. I also hate children.

Sir, I dream of being a mean, unpleasant, inconsiderate bastard! In other words: please give me the chance to drive for Warrington Borough Transport! My recent experience of your bus service was quite the eye opener, as well as opening a gash on my leg and my top lip when sudden braking sent my teeth into the metal handle of the seat in front of me. As an entertainer, I've grown to appreciate the applause of a friendly audience but I now want to hear them scream in terror.

So, could you please send me the forms to apply to become a bus driver for Warrington Borough Transport? I would be eternally grateful and would arrange front row seats at my next performance for you and yours. I guarantee that they're the best seats in the house, as you will see when I throw heavy metal objects at you at random intervals throughout the night.

Come on, can't you move any faster?

Still waiting for a reply. I suppose we'll wait six months and then two will turn up.

STAN MADELEY
THE UK'S TOP RICHARD MADELEY LOOKALIKE
BM NOUMENON, LONDON, WC1N 3XX   EMAIL: STAN@STANMADELEY.COM

The Judging Panel 18th January, 2009
The Caption Competition
The Daily Mail
2 Derry Street
London, W8 5TT

Dear Sir/Madam,

What scam are you villains trying to pull? As a long-time reader and occasional contributor to the *Daily Mail*, I'm shocked that you thought you could get away with it!

I speak, of course, about your recent caption competition (499) in which a jogging David Cameron was shin deep in a pond. I'd thought myself a dead cert for the £20 book token with any of the six suggestions I'd sent to you in a large manila envelope (so large you could hardly have missed it!):

- These shorts are seriously chafing my marginals ...
- I'm not wet, just slightly centre right.
- So, this is how the fox feels.
- Hang on! This isn't champagne!!!
- This is the last time I'm hiring an Olympic standard butler.
- It's like being back at Eton but without all the buggery.

I accept that numbers 1 and 6 might have been a touch too risqué for a family newspaper, but any of the others would have made an excellent winner. Certainly, they would be more worthy of the £20 book voucher than the 'winning' entry submitted by Mr. Royston White of Burgess Hill, West Sussex who offered 'Dare I claim for new trainers on expenses'. How tired and obvious must these captions be? I had explored the expenses scandal but my wife, Sandra (54), suggested that it's now so far out of the news agenda that I shouldn't offer you either 'This pond really needs a duck castle' or 'Third time this week I've dropped the car keys in the moat'. In fact, I have another dozen captions which didn't make the cut but all of which would have shamed Mr. Royston White of Burgess Hill, West Sussex.

Now look here ... I've got nothing against Mr. Royston White of Burgess Hill, West Sussex but if your loyal readers are to take part in these caption competitions, we need to know that it's a fair fight and that the best caption does win. I'd hate to think that this is a scam run by some jaded journalist over a gin-based lunch in a first-card-out-of-the-bowler-hat scenario.

What procedures do you have to ensure that all the entries are read? That the ballot isn't rigged? How can I be sure that you're not Mr. Royston White of Burgess Hill, West Sussex or that Mr. Royston White of Burgess Hill, West Sussex is not one of your in-laws? Do you really think that 'Dare I claim for new trainers on expenses' is funnier than 'These shorts are seriously chafing my marginals'? When I put this very question to a live nightclub audience it provoked such a sense of injustice that there was nearly rioting.

 Your extremely cynical friend in cabaret,

THE DAILY MAIL LONDON

Telegrams, Daily Mail, London, W.8.
Telephone: 020-7938 6000

Northcliffe House,
2 Derry Street,
Kensington,
London, W8 5TT

Dear Mr Madeley,

I assure you all the caption entries are read and not just pulled out of a hat! Better luck next time!

Kind regards, Nicola Tapsell, Assistant to Andy Simpson, Readers Letters Editor.

WITH COMPLIMENTS

GAP OF IMPARTIALITY

They've done it! They've picked another winner!

STAN MADELEY
THE UK'S TOP RICHARD MADELEY LOOKALIKE
BM NOUMENON, LONDON, WC1N 3XX   EMAIL: STAN@STANMADELEY.COM

Ms. Nicola Tapsell
Assistant to Andy Simpson (Readers' Letters Editor)
The Daily Mail
2 Derry Street
London, W8 5TT

3rd February, 2010

Re. Caption Competition (499)

Dear Nicola,

Both wife and self thoroughly enjoyed reading your impassioned defence of the *Daily Mail*'s caption competition but don't think for one moment that we believed a word of it! If it's not a hat you pull the answers from, I suggest it's a sack. And if it's not a sack, I imagine it's a handbag, a wastepaper basket, or the knotted leg of Mr. Quentin Letts' trousered tweed.

Look. We're both wise in the ways of the world. You don't need to come out and tell me that Mr. Royston White of Burgess Hill, West Sussex is a friend of yours. Just tip me the wink and we'll say no more about it. I just wish that I'd known that the quality of the caption entries means nothing before I'd wasted considerable postage sending you my suggestions in a large manila envelope. Are you aware that it cost me nearly a quid?

What you need to do is look at this from my point of view. I am a highly respected entertainer of over twenty-five years in the entertainment business, writing my own material which has never failed to amuse a seaside audience. I sent you half a dozen of my best one-liners including the one that read 'these shorts are seriously chafing my marginals'. Do you honestly expect me to believe that any sane person would think that 'Dare I claim for new trainers on expenses' is funnier? The comedic possibilities of 'marginals' is vast, the word 'chafing' light on the ear, whilst the leadenness of 'seriously' locates the line in a profoundly satiric tradition stretching back to the immortal Alexander Pope.

I think what you need is some kind of independent arbitration.

If it helps, I would be happy to drop into the *Daily Mail* offices each week to help you sort out the entries and to pick a winner. In fact, I will do just that once I get back from my holidays. Wife and self are going for two weeks of tan in Spain starting the 15th February. What do you say to my nipping in sometime during the week of the 1st March and giving it a go? You can show me your hat/sack/wastepaper basket whilst I'm there.

Seriously, Nicola: with a man with extensive comedy experience involved in the process, you could avoid this kind of problem in the future.

Sincerely,

Stan Madeley

CC. Andy Simpson (Readers' Letters Editor)

STAN MADELEY
THE UK'S TOP RICHARD MADELEY LOOKALIKE
BM NOUMENON, LONDON, WC1N 3XX   EMAIL: STAN@STANMADELEY.COM

Mr. Adrian Williams
Managing Director
Pashley Cycles
Stratford-upon-Avon
Warwickshire, CV37 9NL

6th January, 2010

Dear Adrian,

Well, slip your leather seat between my buttocks and call me satisfied!

I'm writing in response to Peter Kay's excellent column in today's *Daily Mail*. Like many right-minded folk, I was distraught when I first heard that supermodel/actress/student Lily Cole has had her bicycle stolen. Imagine, then, my delight when I read that you have generously replaced her bicycle at no cost! The bit that stood out for me was when you said: 'I thought it was rotten to think of Lily losing her Princess, and I didn't want it to spoil her holidays. Plus, Lily looks so gorgeous on the Princess I couldn't bear her being without one.'

Such noblesse, such breeding! This is precisely why I always ride a Pashley!

But here's the strange thing. I was recently astride my own Princess, riding around Manchester where I'm currently performing in cabaret, as well as studying at the University. I've become something of a talking point in my own right when riding down Oxford Road, peddling from nightclub to lecture hall on my Princess. It certainly attracts attention as I often carry 'Wee' Ron Pickins, the famous cabaret nanus, in the basket attached to my handlebars. We're hoping to graduate as arborists later this year.

Anyway, after a fiendishly difficult bark exam, we nipped into the Famous Paddy's Goose, just off Princess Street. We were there to prepare for another exam and compare pruning notes. It was a long study session and, when I carried Pickins out around 1 a.m., we found the Princess gone! All that was left was the bicycle lock with intact combination wrapped around a lamp post. The shock as much as the cold night air worked a miracle on Wee Ron who soon shimmied up the lamp post to see if he could spy my bike off in the distance.

Sadly, even with his perfect eyesight, my diminutive colleague couldn't see the errant velocipede and we were forced to walk back to my rented accommodation where we continued to drown our sorrows in another extended revision session until dawn.

As you can imagine, the loss of my bike has affected me very badly. It was probably the reason why I failed my arboreal exam – a double blow, since I'm considered something of a supermodel/actor/student. Losing my Princess has really spoiled my holidays. Plus, to be honest, I looked so gorgeous on the Princess that I'd be surprised if anybody could bear me to be without one.

As you can tell, this letter is very much apropos of nothing. Just thought I'd batter my baby blues in your direction, show you a little ankle, and hope that you feel that there's something you can do for me. It would be below me as both a gentleman and a tree scholar to suggest that you only give out free bikes to good-looking redheads and/or strawberry blondes.

Your peddleless friend in cabaret,

PASHLEY CYCLES
Masons Road
Stratford-upon-Avon
Warwickshire
CV37 9NL
England

Tel: 01789 292263
Fax: 01789 414201
www.pashley.co.uk
sales@pashley.co.uk

Stan Madeley
BM Noumenon
London
WC1N 3XX

Dear Mr. Madeley,

Adrian has passed me your correspondence regarding your stolen Pashley.

Terrible news!

I'm afraid when it comes to celebrity gift bikes we have a limit of one a decade and Lily seems to have coined in rather early. Not even the Queen herself (please feel free to stand) could prise a freebie out of us until 2020. Sorry about that. We hope you were insured and the malfeasant bike thief is bought to justice.

The root of the problem may have been the lock used. May we suggest branching out and trying some other makes of lock? Some seem to be just for show...their metaphorical bark being worse than their bite. This leaves the potential thief an easy job of stealing your machine. Put a decent lock on the bike and it wood sap even the most entrenched recidivists will to nab your Pashley.

We did enjoy your letter very much. I have enclosed a free brochure, pricelist and stockist list for your perusal.

Best Regards

John Conod

Pashley Holdings Ltd
Reg. No. 02974132 England

STAN MADELEY
THE UK'S TOP RICHARD MADELEY LOOKALIKE
BM NOUMENON, LONDON, WC1N 3XX EMAIL: STAN@STANMADELEY.COM

Nigeria High Commission
9 Northumberland Avenue
London, WC2N 5BC

21st September, 2009

Re.: I want to become Nigerian

Hello, my very dear brothers and sisters!

Allow me to introduce myself. My name is Stanley Madeley (by deed poll) and I am the UK's top Richard Madeley lookalike and the star of 'Hope Breeds Gerbil – The Stanley Madeley Experience Live!', which is currently the top box-office draw across theatres in the whole of Harrow Weald.

This morning I had an email from Mr. Sanusi Lamido Sanusi, Executive Governor of the Central Bank of Nigeria (CBN), who informed me that your government owes me US$10,700,000 for 'contract work'. As I told Mr. Sanusi in the email I sent him (along with my bank details and PIN number), I'm delighted by this windfall. With there being less lookalike work since Mr. Madeley retired to make ornamental crystal pixies, life has been tough in the Madeley home. But not any more! We're drinking Malibu cocktails and it's still only 2.30 in the afternoon!

I must say I was surprised that your government remembered me. It's been nearly eight years since I did that cabaret tour of Nigeria and I have always assumed that it hadn't gone down that well, what with my stomach upsets ruining many of the shows. Anyway, both wife and self are thrilled by this outcome. They always say that it takes time for genius to be recognised and I'm just pleased that you finally recognised my genius to the amount of US$10,700,000.

Now that I'm a multi-millionaire, I was wondering if it would be wise to keep my US$10,700,000 inside Nigeria, to avoid the tax issues involved in transferring it to my Abbey National Savers Account. I'm aware that this would mean that I'd have to become Nigerian. Could you please send me the relevant documents required so that I can adopt Nigerian citizenship? Could you also tell me what kind of perks I'd expect by becoming Nigerian? What kind of lifestyle could I expect to enjoy if I moved to Lagos with US$10,700,000 in the bank? Would I receive a complimentary hat?

Finally, would it be possible for my wife to retain her British citizenship should she also apply to become Nigerian? Personally, I don't care two hoots about my British citizenship! If I'm applying for a Nigerian passport, I want to be 100 per cent Nigerian. The only doubts I have are based on reports I've heard from friends coming from Nigeria who mention arbitrary arrests. Just how arbitrary are these arrests and would they apply to a man with $10,700,000 in the bank?

Thank you in advance for answering my questions and I look forward to your reply. For as it says in our national anthem: 'Help our Youth the truth to know, in love and honesty to grow, and living just and true, great lofty heights attain, to build a nation where peace and justice shall reign!'

Go Nigeria!

Sandra, did you empty our bank account this morning? Only, my life savings seems a lot to spend on a dress...

STAN MADELEY
THE UK'S TOP RICHARD MADELEY LOOKALIKE
BM NOUMENON, LONDON, WC1N 3XX   EMAIL: STAN@STANMADELEY.COM

Ms. Esther Rantzen
Esther 4 Luton!!!
Unit 74/76 Indoor Market
Bedfordshire, LU1 2TA

16th December, 2009

Dear Esther,

I'm a Luton South voter preparing to jump to the winning ship/bandwagon. Last three elections, I've worn the red ribbons of New Labour but now that I've detected that change is in the air, I want to be sure that I'm adorned with the winning rosette. Naturally, I've been edging my way towards the blue corner but your recent campaigning has given me pause to reconsider. My wife, Sandra (54), tells me that you are being very well received in her local hairdressers. My interest is perked. I like to back winners, Esther, and you strike me as the winning type.

But before we get to the hard politics, allow me to introduce myself. The name is Stanley Madeley (by deed poll) and I make my living as the UK's top Richard Madeley lookalike. I am also a Luton South resident, though currently touring with my one-man show, 'Viennese Slicing Wheel – The Stanley Madeley Experience Live!'.

It has always struck me that you are a woman who cares. You've cared about your viewers, your readers, and I believe that you would care passionately about your constituents. However, I am a little worried about your social policies, especially in the area of health and safety, and I politely ask for clarification.

• Can you assure me that you're no supporter of the 'Nanny State'? The common perception is that you'd limit what a man could do with a pair of shears on the top of a wobbly ladder in his own garden.

• Where do you stand on punishing public displays of indecency, such as the recent cases of youths urinating on war memorials? If you're a 'flogger', Esther, it would help win me over.

• Would your election open the floodgates to other celebrities aspiring to power? You're a lovely woman – of that I have no doubt – but I've no time for that Alan Titchmarsh.

• The media are somewhat hostile to you – that rogue, Quentin Letts, seems to have it in for you – so how do you hope to win him over?

• Finally, I have to ask: are the rumours true that you'd like the national anthem changed so it would always be played on the tuba, moving eventually to the full adoption of the theme tune from *That's Life*? I don't want something like that to creep up on me. Full disclosure, Esther. I'm quite happy with 'God Save the Queen'.

I enclose a stamped addressed envelope in the hope that you could direct some campaign literature my way along with your responses to my questions. If you come through for us, both wife and self would be happy to join your campaign (though, to be fair, at the moment, it's Sandra (54) who is the more eager). Wishing you a Merry Christmas and a landslide majority in the New Year.

    Slowly getting on your wavelength!

STAN MADELEY
THE UK'S TOP RICHARD MADELEY LOOKALIKE
BM NOUMENON, LONDON, WC1N 3XX   EMAIL: STAN@STANMADELEY.COM

Esther Rantzen
Esther 4 Luton!!!
Unit 74/76 Indoor Market
Bedfordshire, LU1 2TA

23rd February, 2010

Dear Esther,

It's cold out on that campaign trail so I thought I'd send you socks.

I suppose this is an unusual way to get a local political candidate's attention but I have to tell you the truth, Esther: I'm feeling much less positive about the whole political process this year. You might remember that I wrote to you just before Christmas offering the services of both self and wife, Sandra (54), in your forthcoming electoral campaign. I was full of optimism about your chances and was eager to leap into the winning fray, despite my being stuck up here in Manchester on cabaret business. You must remember that I'd been 'on the fence' as to my sympathies but the favourable impression you've been making on the Luton doorsteps had made me list your way. My wife, I should add, was already there and listing heavily Estherwards.

Well since then, we've heard nothing back from either you or your campaign team. No dates or times of meetings, no mention of early starts in car parks where we'd share flasks of hot Bovril before we'd go leafleting together. Not even a chance to hold back crowds as you tour Luton's shopping centre. This is particularly disappointing because I'm quite good at holding back crowds. I'm a damn good shin kicker, Esther, so you're missing out on the chance to work with one of the best in the business.

What I find particularly disappointing is that you have a chance to endear yourself further with your electorate. I have quite the following and many of my bookings in the coming months are in the Luton area. I could be Bono to your Blair. It could be 1997 all over again. Do you remember D:ream singing 'Things Can Only Get Better'? Well, wait until you hear my version of 'Things Can Only Get Esther'! It's enough to melt a woman's knees, particularly if she's wearing thermal socks.

Speaking of the socks and setting all levity aside: I hope they keep your feet warm. We lose 80% of our body heat through our feet ... or the head. Can't remember which but I'm sure it's one or the other. I'll tell you what: I'll send you a hat next time so we've got both ends covered.

Anyway, I'll end by again repeating that I have thoroughly admired your work over many years and believe there would be no finer prospect for this country than to see you in parliament taking your no-nonsense politics all the way. I'll say no more and hope that you can acknowledge this letter or, at the very least, the socks which I assume won't cause you any problems vis-à-vis the parliamentary ombudsman. I'm told you don't have to declare gifts until you're elected, so perhaps I'll bang the hat in the post for you ASAP.

Your friend in cabaret,

To: stan@stanmadeley.com
From: Esther Rantzen
Date: 03/03/2010 13:43
Subject: Thank you

Dear Stan,

Thank you very much for the socks, It was a kind thought.

Maybe one day you will perform in Luton.

Kind Regards

Esther

Esther Rantzen Luton Advice Office
Units 74/76 Luton Market Hall
Luton Mall
Luton, Beds. LU1 2TA

www.esther4luton.com

Is that it? I mean, is that really it? She'd won me over, Sandra, but now... This is like Su Pollard all over again.

If you need me, I'll be down the pub. And I won't be drinking halves...

STAN MADELEY
THE UK'S TOP RICHARD MADELEY LOOKALIKE
BM NOUMENON, LONDON, WC1N 3XX   EMAIL: STAN@STANMADELEY.COM

Mr. Bryan Magrath   15th February, 2010
Chief Executive Officer
Vision Express UK Ltd
Abbeyfield Road
Lenton

Dear Bryan,

My wife and I are seagoing folk, though my career, as you can see, has been spent landlocked in cabaret with a particular emphasis on my being the UK's top Richard Madeley lookalike. The variety business has certainly served me well and I now find myself in the happy position of having money in the bank and a chance to get out whilst I'm ahead. To be honest, Bryan, I have grown tired of travelling around the country and now intend to retire and settle down in Grimsby with my wife, Sandra (54). We have plans to open a small shop serving the harbour, selling ship-related merchandise such as compasses, life jackets, flares (trousers and rockets), anchors, rations, rudders, flags, rope and cordage. We would like to become the one-stop shopping experience for the busy sailor.

Naturally, we want the business to be a success and we're in the process of producing our marketing material. This includes a large sign for the store front and, here's the clever part, a helium-filled balloon which we will fly above our shop advertising our company name to those on shore and also out at sea.

The reason I'm writing to you is I wanted to be sure that it would be okay with you if we called our venture 'Mizzen Express'. The mizzen, as you will know, is the 'third mast from the bow in a vessel having three or more masts'. Of course, it is the 'after' or 'shorter' mast if you happen to be standing on a yawl, a ketch, or, indeed, a dandy.

Initially, we don't have any plans to expand our operation beyond Grimsby, though if it proved to be a success, I can't rule out a chain of shops in future in other coastal ports. Naturally, we would not be in the eyewear business unless, of course, you count binoculars, telescopes, or sextants. We would sell sunglasses but they would be non-prescription and for nautical use only. Another distinguishing feature of Mizzen Express would be my name and face, which I intend to exploit as much as I can in the early years.

We are aware that you have a store on Newbiggen Walk and for this reason we haven't taken property in Grimsby's main shopping area. Indeed, our business presence in the centre of Grimsby would be non-existent, unless you count our balloon which might be visible above the rooftops.

I hope you will find no problem with our brand name, our balloon, or our exciting plans. Both wife and self are hugely excited by the commercial future of Mizzen Express and only ask that you share our excitement, crack the proverbial bubbly across our hull and send us on our way.

Drinking to your health in rum,

vision express
your eyes, our focus

Our ref: RR JC
Please ask for Mrs Reed

4 March, 2010

Stan Madeley
B M Noumenon
London
WC1N 3XX

Dear Mr Madeley

Re: Mizzen Express

We are in receipt of your letter of 15th February and would apologise for the short delay in responding, but have been giving the matter serious consideration.

In the event we would have no objection to your shop in Grimsby being called "Mizzen Express" provided the following concerns and conditions are satisfied:-

1) The sale of "nautical sunglasses". We suspect it may be impossible to restrict your customers use of the sunglasses once purchased, and therefore we would ask that you undertake never to label such product as "Vision Express" or anything confusingly similar to Vision Express.

2) Written confirmation and undertaking from you that you will not provide ophthalmic services (including eye examinations) within the shop in Grimsby or any other retail outlet.

3) Confirmation and undertaking that you will not open a retail outlet (anywhere in the UK) in a street that already has a Vision Express store on it.

4) Confirmation and undertaking that you will not use Mizzen Express in any style/format which would be considered the same as, or similar to, Vision Express's corporate livery.

5) It is important that you never make reference to Vision Express or any association with us or about your shops, in any advertising and/or promotional activities.

If you can give us the prescribed assurances and undertakings then we would be willing to provide the necessary consents.

We await hearing from you.

Yours sincerely

Rosaleen Reed
Legal Executive & Company Secretary
VISION EXPRESS (UK) LIMITED

S T A N   M A D E L E Y
THE UK'S TOP RICHARD MADELEY LOOKALIKE
BM NOUMENON, LONDON, WC1N 3XX   EMAIL: STAN@STANMADELEY.COM

Ms. Sarah Barrett 9th January, 2010
Head of Customer Experience
Manchester Airport
Manchester, M90 1QX

Dear Ms. Barrett,

I've just finished watching a recent interview of yours and you struck me as an extremely reasonable young woman who would have the sensitivity to understand a celebrity traveller's predicament. You see, I am the UK's top Richard Madeley lookalike and I travel regularly via Manchester to Spain where I perform at some of the country's top tourist nightclubs. As a repeat patron of your airport, I am concerned to learn of the introduction of full body scanners. If the news is to be believed, the system strips a person's body of all clothes and reveals foreign objects hidden about their person.

Let me be quite clear: I fully support your right (indeed, duty) to scrutinise people about to board a plane. I also have absolutely no problem with people seeing me naked. During my twenties and thirties, nudity was a staple part of my act, and the thought of people seeing the older me without clothes is no problem. You might even say that I'm proud of my body. Should your security people wish to strip-search me on the airport concourse, I would not bat an eyelid! I am writing, however, in regard to a personal matter and I hope that you will find no amusement in what follows.

Beyond sending you photographic evidence (which decency forbids), I have no way of explaining why my genitals could be mistaken for a handgun. I am told that the likeness is uncanny. Since I'm not au fait with weapons, I couldn't tell you the make and model, but this similarity has been noted many times – the result of many years spent working as a male stripper, forced to wear tight-fitting thongs for long hours.

Naturally, I am now concerned that travelling via Manchester will become a repeat of my experiences of Gatwick Airport in 2002 when these body scanning systems were first trialled. Back then, I was repeatedly tackled by armed police officers and pinned to the ground whilst my trousers were checked for 'the weapon'.

Can you assure me that my condition will not mark me out for regular searches and will not cause any unnecessary delays? Indeed, would it be possible for me to make other arrangements, perhaps provide documentary evidence or a note from my doctor to explain my unique problem? Alternatively I could make arrangements to undergo a quick body search as soon as I arrive so that you can clear me to board my flight?

It is my wish that you will be able to assure me that my trips to the continent will continue and that holidaymakers will be able to continue to enjoy my family friendly cabaret act.

I remain, your friend in cabaret,

Stanley P. Madeley, Producer & Artist
The Stanley Madeley Experience Live!

manchester airport

Manchester Airport
Olympic House, Manchester M90 1QX United Kingdom
t: + 44 (0) 8712 710 711   f: + 44 (0) 161 489 3813
www.manchesterairport.co.uk

Mr. S. Madeley
BM Noumenon
London
WC1N 3XX

18 January 2010

Dear Mr. Madeley,

Thank you for your letter dated 9th January 2010 regarding Imaging Technology within the airport.

In order to alleviate your concerns about the body scanners that are currently being trialled at Manchester Airport please find enclosed some information which we hope will answer any queries that you may have.

We look forward to welcoming you at Manchester Airport in the near future.

Yours sincerely

Sarah Barrett
Head of Group Customer Experience
Manchester Airports Group

Cc - Daniel King – Customer Relations Manager

MAG

Registered Office: PO Box 532, Town Hall, Manchester, M60 2LA, England, UK. Registered in England No. 1960988
Manchester Airport is a division of Manchester Airport plc.

INVESTOR IN PEOPLE

STAN MADELEY
THE UK'S TOP RICHARD MADELEY LOOKALIKE
BM NOUMENON, LONDON, WC1N 3XX   EMAIL: STAN@STANMADELEY.COM

Mr. Jim McCarthy (Chief Executive)　　　　　　　9th January, 2010
Poundland
Wellmans Road
West Midlands, WV13 2QT

Dear Jim,

After fifteen years on the variety circuit, the last fourteen of those as the top Richard Madeley lookalike in the country, I recently announced my retirement at the Buckingham Folk and Cabaret Festival. Wife and self will soon be moving closer to our children in Luton and we are planning to invest our savings into a new business venture, run by my Sandra (54, a very keen gardener), whilst I enjoy an early retirement and pen my autobiography (publisher pending).

The shop will be selling water features, as well as providing material for people wanting a rich aquatic experience from their gardens. We are thinking of calling the company 'Pondland' and wondered if we'd run into any kind of legal difficulties if we did so. My brother, Paul, has knocked up a graphic for the company and we're currently in the process of having it fabricated. Before I give him permission to have it made into a sixteen-foot sign in illuminated Plexiglass, I thought I'd check with you. Here is the graphic:

Pondland

As you can see, the font and colour are uniquely our own (note our rich aquamarine blue) and are unlikely to be mistaken for your excellent store. I think that to even the most causal observer, it's obvious that we're in the pond business and have no connection with Poundland, especially since your closest branch would be in the Luton Arndale Centre, some few hundred years away from our proposed site.

Regarding our trading: we won't be competing with you on price. There will be very little in our shop that's priced at a pound (though I can't promise that the pound price-point will be uniquely your own!) Also, the majority of our goods will be pond related – aquatic plants, filtration systems, books on how to encourage wildlife, ornamental plastic herons. That sort of thing ...

I hope you appreciate that we would not move forward with our plans without consulting you and I eagerly anticipate what I'm sure will be an enthusiastic response. And rest assured that if you ever find yourself in the market for cheap pond liner, you and your collegues on the Board of Directors would receive a healthy discount in 'Pondland'!

　　　　　　I remain, your friend in cabaret,

Poundland®

Mr Stan Madeley
BM Noumenon
London
WC1N 3XX

Your ref:
Our ref: JJ/IP/Misc

3rd February 2010

Dear Mr Madeley

Request to approve use of Pondland

Thank you for your letter dated 12th January 2010.

I have discussed your request with our in-house solicitor before responding.

While I wish you and your wife every success in your new venture I regret that I an unable to agree to your request for the reasons set our below.

Our company has been trading under this well recognised brand for over 20 years and we own several registered trade marks for the mark, Poundland. Since trading commenced in 1991 the company has accrued a considerable amount of goodwill in this brand, so much so that while the name you suggest is not identical, it is nevertheless sufficiently similar as to be likely to cause confusion to potential customers. And this could be confusion not only to Poundland customers but also your potential customers.

Furthermore, as you may be aware, we also sell fish related items such as fish food, nets, fish tanks and other fish-related paraphernalia which is likely to add further confusion.

I am therefore unable to confirm my consent to the use of the name Pondland as set out in your letter and hope that you will appreciate why this is the case. Nevertheless I appreciate your honesty in the matter and wish you every success.

Yours sincerely
**For and on behalf of
POUNDLAND LIMITED**

**J McCarthy
Chief Executive**

Poundland Limited, Wellmans Road
Willenhall, West Midlands WV13 2QT, UK

Telephone: +44 (0)121 568 7000
Fax: +44 (0)121 568 7007
www.poundland.com

Registered in England Company No: 2495645. Registered Office: Wellmans Road, Willenhall, West Midlands WV13 2QT

STAN MADELEY
THE UK'S TOP RICHARD MADELEY LOOKALIKE
BM NOUMENON, LONDON, WC1N 3XX   EMAIL: STAN@STANMADELEY.COM

His Holiness, Pope Benedict XVI 31st January, 2010
Apostolic Palace
00120 Vatican City

Dear Most Holy Father,

It was with the profoundest shock that I witnessed the terrible news footage from Christmas of that poor misguided woman launching herself at you. And if you don't mind my saying: I think a few self-defence classes wouldn't go amiss! My wife, Sandra (54), could show you a couple of Aikido hip throws that would have had that sinner on her knees quicker than prayer, though I can't say that it would do as much for her soul. Of course, we watched the coverage on Sky News rather than the BBC. Ever since Jane Hill admitted to what she does with her weekends, I find that I can't watch News 24 with my supper. However, it was interesting to see that you've now forgiven your assailant and that is precisely the reason why I am now writing at half past four in the morning.

You are perhaps the world's leading opponent to moral relativism, which I have also been attacking in my own small way through my stage shows (I'm a cabaret entertainer by trade). And as I'm sure you're finding: changing people's perceptions is not easy! They tell me that I'm old-fashioned because I believe in good manners, education, a strong army, protecting our borders, monogamy, loving thy neighbour, paying your way, metal trouser zips, keeping the lawn cut, not doling money out to beggars, saving for a rainy day, and tinkering as little as possible with nature. Same sex marriages just don't do it for me, I'm afraid, but I'm also uncertain about 99 per cent of the villains who turn up at our local registry office looking to have their passports endorsed via a sham betrothal.

I am writing to ask you then: where does forgiveness feature in the argument against moral relativism? What is moral relativism if it's not a form of universal forgiveness? The moral landscape used to be defined by its high peaks, deep valleys, and occasional middling planes where most of us live and sin. We are now stuck in a land with no elevation and where everything is permitted. Essentially, we're stuck in the Netherlands. And, as you know, the Netherlands is not known for its moral philosophers. Except Erasmus, of course. And Spinoza. Hugo Grotius too, I suppose . . . But even if the Netherlands is known for its philosophers, they have yet to come up with a compelling argument in favour of forgiveness towards my neighbour who has trimmed her conifers and deliberately dumped the clippings on our side of the fence.

It is so hard to love one's neighbours! I don't know if you have this problem in the Holy City but people have taken to parking on the grass verge outside our house. It's difficult to retain one's faith in people when they cut up the turf as they do. It's particularly bad in rainy weather when the ground is soft. Personally, I believe the council should prosecute but you know what councils are like. They never listen! Well, the Vatican Council, you might answer, but you've not had one of those since 1965. I want action this day, as Churchill used to say.

I will end by saying that I'm delighted that you've brought this subject up for popular debate (such as this letter) and hope that you continue to fight the good fight on behalf of virtuous men and women around the world. Without doubt, you are already my favourite Pope.

Per Angusta Ad Augusta,

SECRETARIAT OF STATE

FIRST SECTION · GENERAL AFFAIRS

From the Vatican, 2 March 2010

Dear Mr Madeley,

The Holy Father has received your letter and he has asked me to send you this acknowledgement. His Holiness will pray for you and your wife Sandra and he sends you his blessing.

Yours sincerely,

Monsignor Peter B. Wells
Assessor

Mr Stanley Madeley
BM Noumenon
LONDON
WC1N 3XX

STAN MADELEY
THE UK'S TOP RICHARD MADELEY LOOKALIKE
BM NOUMENON, LONDON, WC1N 3XX EMAIL: STAN@STANMADELEY.COM

Cooking Vinyl
10 Allied Way
London, W3 0RQ

22nd February, 2010

How's it crackin' my Bro?

I'm doing a shout out to the fans of the number one frosty fella, Mr. Stanley Madeley (by deed poll), down here in the hood in the grime town of Luton on ma home turf of Bedfordshire.

I'm putting down lyrics to say to yous that me and thee can make sweet music together. Keepin it real, I don't hose bull in a drive-by of disrespect when I say that in the scene you are the Kings of Knees to the Queen B. You is knocking fellas so why don't we make the yayo together with an album that is off the hinges? Being the tops in the biz, you are repped high and can bust me out to the peeps on the street. But allow me to ID the self. It's the yard where the name is Mr. Stan and he is the UK's top Richard Madeley lookalike. This ice cream ain't no vanilla!

What am I selling? Just the sound of the mack daddy. I got my ride iced up and my phat stitch, Sandra (54), is at my side shaking it loose with the jive honey. She is stunning and stubby and our new record is smokin'. We thought we'd give you the word to slip me skin and you get the chance of popping ma cherry the very first time for some network play.

This album is hot. It's hardcore. It is street. It is hip-hop and happening. It is the debut from Stan Madeley, the beefy geeza. We've been stacking cheese for months to put the green lizard down on this cut. I ain't about to split no lip to say this is the best 12 inch of dog mustard you've ever spooned into your ears. I've izzled my schnozzle, ma ho drizzling, dizzying, and whizzling, ma Victoria sponge is the schizzle.

So that's it. All cracking and a lackin and Joe Blow is sound. So, don't forget the name. It's the Stan Sound, the D of the O of the G. It's the sound of the hound. Stan Madeley, rockin' the gold. My smile is carat and I'm livin' nappy.

Keep it big, King Cone. Stay slick cos I have the Big Willie style.

I enc. a freshly minted envelope from the self-seal scene. Don't diss the man. I ain't no poodle. I ain't no noodle. Smell me well and slide me a little respect with paper back.

Word.

Sincerely yours,

Yo yo yo, Missy S (54)! No word? Dawg! I peeled that prune. Now I'm bum cracking mince about it.
STANLEY M

```
S  T  A  N     M  A  D  E  L  E  Y
THE UK'S TOP RICHARD MADELEY LOOKALIKE
BM NOUMENON, LONDON, WC1N 3XX    EMAIL: STAN@STANMADELEY.COM
```

Mr. Clive James
c/o Robert Kirby
12-26 Lexington Street
London, W1F 0LE

4th September, 2009

Dear Mr. James,

Allow me to introduce myself. My name is Stanley Madeley (by deed poll) and I am the UK's top Richard Madeley lookalike and widely recognised as an expert in the field of communicative dance. You might remember me from one of your recent shows at the Edinburgh Fringe (I was sat on the front row to the right of the stage) where both wife and self had a thoroughly good time, ending with a fish supper on Roseneath Street.

I am writing to you about something that occurred to me during your performance. The halibut pie was still but a gleam in my wife's eye and you were up on stage, making a quip about sling-backed sandals, if I recall. It was then that my attention began to roam. I might add that there was nothing wrong with your appearance. I would even go so far as to commend you for the inch of naked ankle visible between sock and trouser. 'Twas très risqué. And the audience was clearly spellbound by your wit and anecdotes. Yet I couldn't help but feel that the place lacked a certain dynamism. It was clear to me as a professional choreographer that something was missing. Then it struck me like holy revelation: your show would benefit enormously from a troupe of dancing girls lined up behind you in tassels, corsets, thongs, and crotchless stockings. They worked for the late George Burns and I see them working for you, perhaps one on each arm (or leg, if you prefer).

So strong was this epiphany that I have taken the liberty of putting your poem 'A Gesture Towards James Joyce' to a popular show tune and my highly trained chorus line is on 24 hours notice to perform it at a location of your choosing in the Greater London area. The girls come from across Europe and have experience working in UK theatres, festivals, community centres, strip joints, speakeasies, universities, carveries and bars. As you can see by the attached illustration, the concept works extremely well. I hope you don't mind but I've taken the additional liberty of branding them 'The Clive James Dancers' on your behalf. (You might think the branding cruel and unnecessarily painful but I have found it necessary given the demand for well-endowed stunners over six feet in the highly competitive and gangster-dominated market of people smuggling. It's always better to have them marked as ours!)

I look forward to hearing from you and hope that you fully appreciate how important you now are in the lives of twenty five girls who have not enjoyed a good break since slipping from the freight wagons in Dover. Enclosed is a signed photo of self as a sign of goodwill towards thee.

Best wishes,

[signature]

> Sandra, I'll be in bed crying over my copy of 'Cultural Amnesia'... Like Cocteau's admirers, my mistake was to 'imagine that novelty was an ethos'...
> (Cultural Amnesia, p. 132)

STAN MADELEY
THE UK'S TOP RICHARD MADELEY LOOKALIKE
BM NOUMENON, LONDON, WC1N 3XX   EMAIL: STAN@STANMADELEY.COM

Transformations
413 Bury Old Road
Manchester, M25 1PS

5th February, 2010

Dear Sir and/or Madam,

I am not myself transgender but I share a dressing room with a man who is!

Allow me to introduce myself. The name is Stanley Madeley (by deed poll) and although I am the UK's top Richard Madeley lookalike, I'm currently working the cruise ship cabaret circuit here in the Med (my wife will be posting this, possibly from Leeds or Manchester). As you might imagine, sword swallowing at sea is highly stressful work but to compensate I currently have a dressing room to myself. I normally share the room with another cabaret performer but Terry is currently enjoying a much-deserved six-week break after working Christmas and the New Year. You should know that he has a very convincing drag act which has made him hugely popular with the geriatric cruise audience.

Since Terry is away, I have been alone for long hours in this cabin. Professionally I am going through a difficult time. I've been working on a new cabaret show which is called 'Pituitary Loft Escalation – The Stanley Madeley Experience Live!' which is a little too surreal for the geriatric cruise audience. The stress has been terrible! Being inquisitive of nature, I found myself rather bored the other evening and I began to examine Terry's silicone breasts pads which, I'll be perfectly honest, I found utterly fascinating. Each time I came off stage, I would return to the pads to give them a squeeze. I don't know if you're aware of this but they are very therapeutic. You could sell them as some kind of stress relief!

Anyway, to cut a long story short, I am now at the point where the pads are completely destroyed and I need to source replacements before Terry comes back from his holiday. I've traced one of the pads onto the attached sheet and would be extremely grateful if you could price me replacements based on the dimensions. My wife, Sandra (54), will order them and see that they are delivered when we next dock in Gibraltar. Naturally, the pads were rounder than they appear in my drawing and not quite as flat but, as you can see, I've really mangled them! However, I hope this will give you a good idea as to Terry's cup size.

I can't stress the worry that this is causing me. Terry is six feet four inches tall, hails from Glasgow, and can get furious if he even loses just an eyelash.

Your friend currently off the coast of North Africa,

Transformation

Our Ref BBD/CDC   10.02.10

Stanley Madeley
BM Noumenon
London
WC1N 3XX

Dear Stanely

Thank you for your letter which we have received today.

We do stock various silicone breasts which can be seen on our website www.transformation.co.uk but looking at the shape you have traced we do not stock anything like this.

I can tell you that silicone breast forms are very hardy and rarely split or become mishapen, however, this will depend on how long your friend has had them.

Without seeing an actual picture of the form I am unable to advise but you may see something suitable on our website. If there is something that ressembles the damaged forms then please contact me as soon as possible and I will be happy to help.

Hope to hear from you soon

Kind regards

Beverley
Customer Service Department

The World's Leading TV Specialists

Head Office: 407 Bury Old Road, Prestwich, Manchester, UK, M25 1PS
Telephone: (UK)   0161 773 4477   Fax: 0161 773 6358
Telephone: (Overseas) ++44 161 773 4477   Fax: ++44 161 773 6358
Shops in London, Bristol, Birmingham, Manchester, Newcastle, Dublin, Frankfurt and Berlin.
Directors: Stephanie Anne Lloyd, R. Ristic, D.A. Booth, S.A. Booth.
A division of the Mapleleaf Holdings Group - registered in England No. 215082

```
S  T  A  N     M  A
THE UK'S TOP   RICHARD M
BM NOUMENON, LONDON, WC1N 3XX    EMA
```

> Sandra, at this point, do something to remind readers that David Dimbleby was famously knocked over by a bullock.

Sir David Dimbleby

Dear David,

I've just been reading in today's *Daily Mail* about your problems and I wanted to write to tell you that there's no shame in it, lad. I'm 86 years old and I've had bollock trouble since I was in my late fifties. And do you know what? I don't miss either one of em! Gives me more time to read books and I learned to play the harmonica when I was 65 so I don't see why you can't do the same.

I mean a good-looking man like you has nothing to worry about. I worked in cabaret for twenty-nine years and all them goings-on that happens in showbiz was nothing short of disgusting even if I don't suppose it's changed much and I bet it hasn't. But if you ask me, you're better off without all that doing with the fairer sex. Old Sam Powell wouldn't have a bit of it when he was running his troupe back in 1956. I saw him run a girl out of the Hammersmith theatre for interfering with the ventriloquist. Funniest thing I ever saw. Do you know that in them days we had to lock our dressing rooms and we could entertain no female guests after the show? I hope you have the same rules on *Question Time*. Not that I'm saying you have any trouble of that sort, David, but some of your guests look proper sorts. I know that I was as good-looking as that Michel Portillo I'd be very popular with the ladies. My wife Sandra (73) still says he would have made a good Prime Minister. What do you think? I don't trust a man who listens to Wagner.

Anyway, my son-in-law is coming to see us soon so I'll have him post this on his travels. I have had an envelope printed out just in case you want to ask me any advice or just want to chat. I've even got a stamp from my wife's purse. Sandra would like a photo of you but I don't believe in that celebrity nonsense. Trevor's a good lad. Bought me this laptop and a printer. He works for British Telecom so we get the broadbank intranet for free on wireless.

Just remember that there's no shame in it, lad. Keep your chin up even if nothing else works. That's what the ladies like to see more than anything down there. A good sense of humour will take you further than anything in this world. Take it from an old fellow who knows.

Hope you don't mind my writing to you. Would you kindly do more programmes about hills?

Very best wishes,

21/2/10

Dear Mr Madeley

I enjoyed your letter. We all did. As I suspect you knew it was bullocks not bollocks that caused the problem. The latter are fine, so the harmonica will have to wait.

We had your near namesake Richard Madeley on GT just after yr. letter arrived. Coincidence? Or maybe not.

Oh — what _is_ BM Noumenon?

v. best wishes

David Dimbleby

STAN MADELEY
THE UK'S TOP RICHARD MADELEY LOOKALIKE
BM NOUMENON, LONDON, WC1N 3XX   EMAIL: STAN@STANMADELEY.COM

Mr. David Dimbleby   24th February, 2010

Dear David,

I've not enjoyed making a bollock joke this much since Frost's interview with Menachem Begin around 1977 when he wore a pair of his ridiculously flared hipster jeans riding high in the crotch.

I feel that I should apologise, however, for making such an obvious crack at the expense of you and your bullock, though it was my wife, Sandra (actually 54), who suggested that I write. Sometimes one has to go with the material at hand and the opportunity of your bullock incident was too good for either of us to pass up. In my previous letter, I might also have implied that I was a little older than I really am, but, to tell you the truth, the joke wouldn't have worked if you knew that I'm really the UK's top Richard Madeley lookalike. 'Ah!' you would have thought to yourself, 'surely not *the* Stan Madeley?' Well, yes: it is really me. It's a cross I must bear and a particularly heavy one at that, covered with sharp edges and a few protruding corners. The name is Stanley Madeley (by deed poll) and I make a humble but honest living travelling the UK with my ingenious mix of cabaret: stage hypnotism, stoats in a sack, making balloon animals from real balloons and real animals.

The fact that my namesake and lookalike, Mr. Richard Madeley, appeared on *Question Time* was as much a surprise to me as my letter clearly was to you. If I'd known I was going to take away some of his limelight, I would never have written. As to his remarks vis-à-vis Iraq: I would go so far as to say that he knows as much about international politics as I know about cabaret. Read into that what you like.

You ask what is 'B.M. Noumenon'? It is merely the name I chose for my PO Box, though I would have thought you've read enough Kant to know that 'noumenon' is that object constructed by the mind of something as it is in itself and not as it is understood through perception. I suppose it's hard to describe to the layman versed in neither philosophy nor cabaret. It's really an epistemological question much like: 'is it easier for a camel to pass through the eye of a needle than Gordon Brown to appear on *Question Time*?' Though I suppose Kant would have been as stumped as the rest of us about that particular nut.

Speaking of nuts: I am, of course, delighted to learn that you're fine where it matters. I also hope that the bullock is also recovered. In all the media coverage, the poor animal's welfare was clearly forgotten. But isn't that the way with the media? Unless you're a name, you're nobody.

Allow me to end by again asking for more shows about hills, paintings, and poetry (Paxman's *The Victorians* was but a pale and bitter copy of *A Picture of Britain*). By coincidence (or perhaps not), your letter arrived with yet another reply from *The Poetry Review* rejecting my verse. However, your kind words have inspired me to write new lines which I'll be sending to the *Review* with the morning post. I attach my poem to this letter in the hope that you'll accept the dedication of my rhyming best.

Your friend in cabaret,

An Ode on Bullocks
For Mr. David Dimbleby

by Stan Madeley

If bullocks were made to pay a licence fee
(For radio, of course, since they don't watch TV)
One could excuse their grievous actions of late,
When refusing to walk up a trailer's gate.
If it were Paxman giving a cruel prod
You'd expect it given he's a rather rude sod,
But Dimbleby (David), that's a different matter,
No prodder he, just a master of chatter.
But then looking from a bullock's *Point of View*
(Now hosted by Terry Wogan on BBC2)
How would a *Question Time* guest react
If they were regularly spanked across the back,
Ordered to go here and poked to go there,
Told what to eat and then what to wear?
You answer: just like a Tory? Oh, I suppose,
And bullocks might vote for Michael Gove,
Who though forty-one, acts septuagenarian
And forget bullocks: he could be crushed by a hen!
But back to my point, which was quite keen:
It's like bullocks have never seen a TV screen,
For if they had, they'd choose targets no higher,
Than Humphrys (John) or that George Alagiah.

STAN MADELEY
THE UK'S TOP RICHARD MADELEY LOOKALIKE
BM NOUMENON, LONDON, WC1N 3XX EMAIL: STAN@STANMADELEY.COM

The Top Potato
Spudulike
Central Business Centre
Great Central Way
London, NW10 0UR

17th February, 2010

Dear Sir/Madam,

Having made a successful career in cabaret and the celebrity lookalike racket, I will be retiring this year to Nunnykirk in Northumberland where my wife and I own a small freehold. There we grow organic potatoes but we now aim to move into the retail market with a series of franchised operations run by relatives. I don't mind boasting that my wife, Sandra (54), is something of a culinary genius and has now developed a new confection made from boiled potato.

The actual product is frozen onto a stick and we can present it to consumers in the form of a popsicle or as a healthy alternative to ice cream. We are currently looking for celebrity endorsements and I am using my contacts in the entertainment business to see if we can get Gary Wilmot's face on the box.

Our first stall is due to open ahead of the summer season on May 17 and we wondered if your company would have any problem with our branding our product 'Spud-U-Lick'. Naturally, we have nothing to do with baked potatoes and it's clear from our packaging that our product is meant to be licked.

Our marketing will also make it quite clear that we're not spudulike and we're happy to put a small asterisk ('*') at the end of our name which would direct the reader's eye to the small print at the bottom: 'We have nothing to do with spudulike'. This way, we will make it explicit that we are unconnected to your excellent baked potatoes. If this is okay with you, we will move forward with our branding exercise and have signs made for the businesses.

This brings me to a second question. Would you be interested in selling the Spud-U-Lick popsicles in branches of spudulike? With Spud-U-Lick, there's very little preparation needed, little or no litter, and it will bring customers into your shops in the slow season. If you're anything like other food retailers, you will struggle to sell baked potatoes during the hottest months of the year. But with Spud-U-Lick, there's no such problem. It takes over where the baked potato season ends.

I trust that this will be okay and I look forward to sending you some of our lovely iced spud confection as soon as we've sorted out the teething problems and have the operation up and running.

Breaking new ground in potato-based retail,

Jensen & Son

Patent and Trade Mark Attorneys

Established 1867

366-368 Old Street, London EC1V 9LT

T: +44 (0)20 7613 0280   F: +44 (0)20 7613 0267
E: mail@jensens.co.uk   www.jensens.co.uk

Stan Madeley
BM Noumenon,
London
WC1N 3XX

2nd March 2010

Our Ref: M11293

Dear Sirs,

SPUDULIKE Trade Marks

We act in trade mark matters for Spudulike Group Limited of 9 Central Business Centre, Great Central Way, London, NW10 0UR, who are proprietors of *inter alia* European Community Trade Mark No. 2122869 for SPUDULIKE, which registration covers food products made from potatoes in Class 29. Our client takes the protection of their brand and trade marks extremely seriously and has forwarded a letter to us regarding your plans to launch the Spud-U-Lick frozen potato products.

We have advised our client that such a product sold under this trade mark will be a clear infringement of their registered trade mark. Moreover, your offer to specifically exclude any connection to our client is not sufficient to eradicate the likelihood of confusion on the part of the public, which includes the likelihood of association.

In the circumstances, our client would be grateful if you would refrain from using SPUDULICK or any other name similar to their registered trade mark. Our client reserves its rights in all other aspects of this matter.

We look forward to hearing from you.

Yours faithfully,

Jensen & Son

DEREK MOORE CPA EPA MITMA   DAVID S. MOORE BSc (Dunelm) CPA EPA MITMA Patent Agent Litigator

assisted by: Damian Latif BA (Hons) LLM

consultant: John Claisse BSc PhD CPA EPA   systems administrator: Eugenia Varnier BA (Hons)

patent administrator: Alex Schabel   trade mark administrator: Su Newton   accounts manager: Anne Stamp

VAT NO. GB333 363 475

STAN MADELEY
THE UK'S TOP RICHARD MADELEY LOOKALIKE
BM NOUMENON, LONDON, WC1N 3XX   EMAIL: STAN@STANMADELEY.COM

The Guild of Taxidermists
c/o Lancashire County Museums
Stanley Street
Preston, PR1 4YP

23rd February, 2010

Dear Sir,

I'm absolutely new to the world of taxidermy, though my wife, Sandra (54), has been an amateur in the field for a number of years. My business is really cabaret and the celebrity lookalike circuit, and you might have noticed that I have an uncanny (though hopefully flattering) resemblance to Mr. Richard Madeley. What is less obvious is that I'm in the process of retiring and I'm looking to spend more time pursuing a hobby. Naturally, with my wife having an interest in taxidermy, it hasn't taken much for me to also catch the taxidermy bug (though, I hasten to add, I didn't stuff and mount it!)

Seriously, though, with my interest developing, my wife and I have decided to attend our very first UK taxidermy conference. Since I'm currently performing in the North West, we'll be at The Hayes Conference Centre in Swanwick, Derbyshire in a couple of weeks to see Alexander Sokolov mounting a fox. It's a wonderful coincidence that you've invited Mr. Sokolov to our first conference since we watched him mount a moose in his studios on our recent holiday to St. Petersburg. Indeed, it was his stunning work that finally inspired me to try my hand at taxidermy. I recently finished my first vole and I could finally see what my wife has been on about all these years!

However, the reason I'm writing is that we're quite eager to get involved in 'The Avian Challenge' competition. As I said, my wife is an experienced hand (cats, garden birds, badgers, and an owl) but has thus far only displayed her work to friends and family. Her only professional commission was a tortoise and, to be honest, that didn't turn out too well and has quite turned her off reptiles. That said, she does love stuffing birds and wants to do well in the avian competition at this year's conference. If we understand the rules correctly, we must try to copy the pose of the European Jay pictured on your website. We had taken this to mean that we didn't need to use a real European Jay, though it has now been pointed out that the opposite might be implied by the instruction.

To tell you the truth, I think it's very unclear as to whether we're meant to stuff a European Jay or any songbird substituting for a European Jay. As it happens, my wife has spent a month working on a large blackbird we managed to source locally and she has the pose nailed on, though I hasten to add that she didn't use nails (joke!).

Anyway, could you please advise us as soon as possible as to what we should do? Would it be okay to bring her blackbird along? My experience in these things is that there's always some smart arse who has actually found and stuffed a real European Jay. If that is going to influence the judging, we can't see much point in bringing our blackbird, even if it is well mounted. Looking forward to some clarification.

Your friend in cabaret,

Sorry to use your own letter to reply, no headed to hand. The Avian challenge is for a JAY as found in UK & Europe. JAY only as in the picture. Good luck and hope to see you. — James Dickinson.

How Not To Stuff A Jay To Competition-Standard

Step 1. Stuff a blackbird.

Step 2. Buy the paints for an Airfix model of a Russian Mig 35 fighter.

Step 3. Paint the blackbird to the authentic colour scheme of a jay.

Step 4. On the morning of the contest, go shopping instead.

STAN MADELEY
THE UK'S TOP RICHARD MADELEY LOOKALIKE
BM NOUMENON, LONDON, WC1N 3XX   EMAIL: STAN@STANMADELEY.COM

Mr. Sherlock Holmes 　　　　　　　　　　　　　　　　30th September, 2009
221b Baker Street
London, NW1 6XE

Mr dear Mr. Holmes,

Allow me to introduce myself. My name is Stanley Madeley (by deed poll) and I am the UK's top Richard Madeley lookalike, appearing in cabaret nightly with my one-man show, 'Hampstead Knocking Services – The Stanley Madeley Experience Live!'. I was given your address by a man with a limp in his right leg and ginger eyebrows. He recommended your services most highly, though I'm afraid that my troubles might seem rather trivial to a man of your standing.

If you know me at all, you will be aware that I am something of an amateur sleuth. I was intimately involved in 'The Case of The Nigerian with the Hairy Lip' which baffled some of the finest brains in Scotland Yard for months. In the end, it was, as I'd deduced, a moustache. However, this new case has me quite baffled.

I recently appeared on stage with my new act which involves some felicitous conjuration involving tortoises. Naturally, this has led to some unpleasantness with members of the animal rights brigade who dislike my use of tortoises in what is basically a variation of the magic cups/Find the Lady routine. So far there has been nothing more than noisy protests outside the theatre. However, when I returned to my dressing room last night, I discovered that the rucksack in which I keep my tortoises had been emptied. All my tortoises are now missing. Then, this morning, I discovered a piece of paper shoved under my door. It contained the following strange hieroglyph which has thus far defied my analysis.

I fear there is something sinister going on, Mr. Holmes, and I would be very grateful if I could come and see you in Baker Street to discuss the mystery. I trust that Dr. Watson is well. I could do with consulting him too but on a personal matter that requires a prescription ointment.

I look forward to your immediate reply, aware that you are a man with a great reputation in the field of stolen tortoises. I'm sure you will take no time in cracking this code and solving this case.

　　　　　Sincerely yours,

PS. Please ensure that Dr. Watson is there when I arrive. I really do need that ointment.

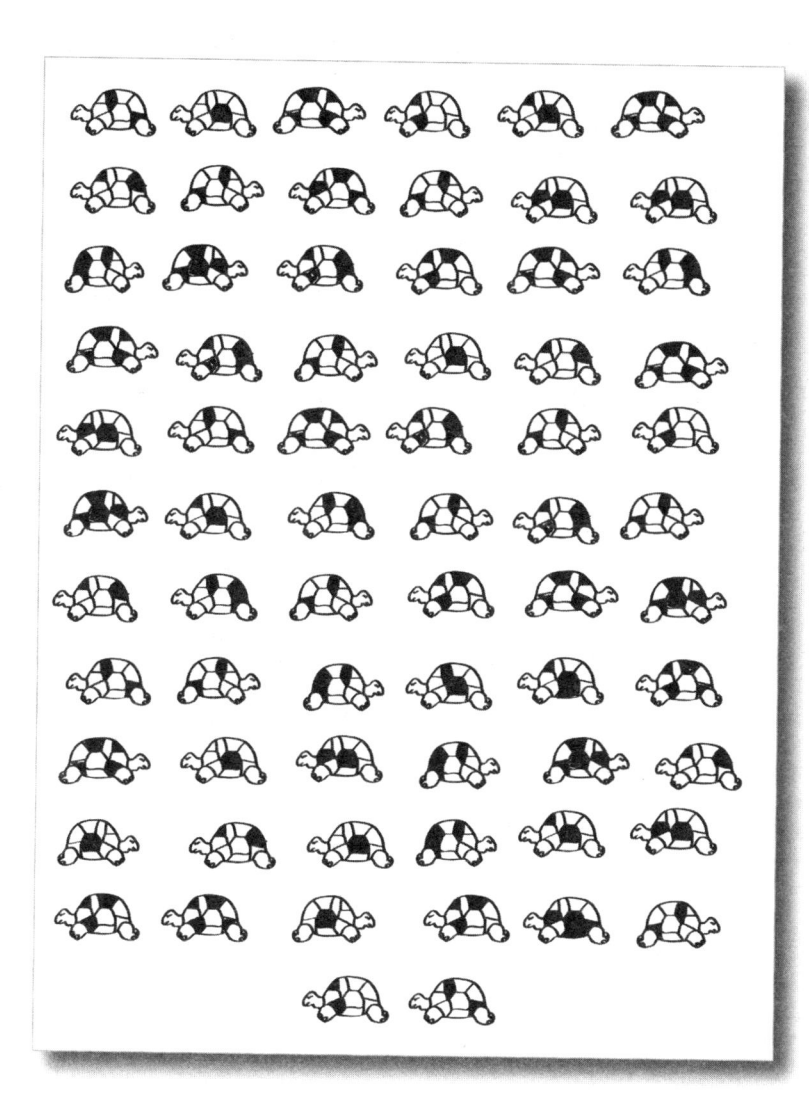

Damn that Holmes!

I'd have more chance if I asked his brother Eamonn.

= A

STAN MADELEY
THE UK'S TOP RICHARD MADELEY LOOKALIKE
BM NOUMENON, LONDON, WC1N 3XX   EMAIL: STAN@STANMADELEY.COM

Building Manager
One Canada Square
Canary Wharf
London, E14 5AB

22nd February, 2010

Dear Sir/Madam,

It is my intention to scale the outside of One Canada Square before the end of July and I wondered if you can advise me as to the relevant parties I need to contact to ensure that this will be a successful and (importantly) lawful attempt to break the UK free-climbing record.

As you might be aware, I have a growing reputation as one of the UK's most talented acts in the area of extreme cabaret. I have already taken my resemblance to TV star Richard Madeley to new heights (pun intended) by scaling some of the tallest structures in Leeds, Mold, Norwich and Kidderminster. I am now transferring my show to the West End and intend to raise public awareness by undertaking a stunt that will be the 'talk of the town'.

Let me assure you from the outset that unlike other free-climbers, my safety is assured by unique equipment developed over fifteen years of scaling glass structures. I have a specially made suit which allows me to adhere to any surface. It excretes industrial-strength epoxy glue, which is stored in a backpack. One canister should be enough for me to scale all 770 feet of your magnificent tower but for safety reasons I will be carrying two. The glue is soluble in rainwater and the slight trail I leave behind me will wash off the glass in a matter of hours. My reputation for scaling impossible heights has already earned me my nickname 'Stan the Slug', though I can assure you that I look better than my name suggests once I slip into my green latex body suit.

Naturally, I would hope to have the media in attendance during the eight-hour climb. I would be commenting throughout my attempt via radio as well as conducting media interviews and Twittering on my new Twitter account (@stanmadeley). My crew, led by my wife, Sandra (54), will be providing logistical support within the building, moving to each floor to monitor my progress. The only requirement they would ask of your staff is an open window every twenty-five floors, through which I will be able to facilitate my natural ablutions into my wife's sanitary bucket.

To ensure the speedy organisation of this event, can I suggest that we aim to hold my first attempt to reach the summit on Tuesday, 1st June? I hope that you will be on board to help me attain my next big dream and look forward to meeting you in the near future to discuss other aspects of the climb that might concern you. This should be a glorious day for One Canada Square, London, and the free-climbing community of the UK.

Your friend in cabaret,

Stan Madeley

CANARY WHARF
GROUP PLC

15 March 2010

Dear Stan

Thank you for your letter dated 22 February 2010 addressed to the Building Manager, One Canada Square. Unfortunately we are unable to provide access to the interior or exterior of the building for this purpose.

Yours Sincerely,

Hamish McDougall

STAN MADELEY
THE UK'S TOP RICHARD MADELEY LOOKALIKE
BM NOUMENON, LONDON, WC1N 3XX EMAIL: STAN@STANMADELEY.COM

Torture Garden
TG Productions Ltd
111 Cremer Business Centre
37 Cremer St
London, E2 8HD

7th November, 2009

Dear Torturers,

Allow me to introduce myself. My name is Stanley Madeley (by deed poll) and I am the UK's top Richard Madeley lookalike and the writer, director and star of the stage musical 'Grievous Bodily Mop – The Stanley Madeley Experience Live'. I also have a rubber Thunderbirds fetish.

I know you probably get a hundred letters like this each week wanting more details on your club's activities for rubber Thunderbirds fetishists and you no doubt have a standard reply/leaflet. However, I require some quite specific details. I have spent the past 15 years living with my secret and only told my wife, Sandra (54), about it six years ago. Thankfully, she's been quite happy to take command of 'Thunderbird 1', as we like to call it, and dress in the full Thunderbirds rubberised outfit two nights a week. We have now got it down to an art and I've even installed an ingenious system of rails and pulleys into the bedroom ceiling that allow her to move around the room while connected to strings. It really does complete the illusion. I call it 'SuperMarionetteMotion'.

I noticed among your website's photographs that you attract a few fellow fans of the Thunderbirds but I was wondering:

• Are we allowed to 'be ourselves' in your club? For instance, would I be allowed to land Thunderbird 1 on 'Tracy Island' or would this get you into trouble with the police?

• Does your club permit entry to non-rubberised Thunderbirds non-fetishists? I don't like to sound too choosy but one of my greatest 'turn-offs' is a Brains lookalike. Though he's handy with a screwdriver and played an integral part to the TV series, he doesn't really connect with my rubberised Thunderbirds vibe and plays no significant part in my sex life.

• Would it be possible to install 'SuperMarionetteMotion' in your club if I could guarantee that our strings would never get tangled and it passes all the Health & Safety regulations?

• Is there room in your club for associated fetishes? I'm thinking, of course, about a rubberised Captain Scarlett, rubberised Stingray, rubberised Fireball XL5, or a rubberised Joe 90. I do occasionally like to dress as a rubberised Captain Troy Tempest whilst my wife adopts the guise of a rubberised Aquaphibian. Perhaps we could organise themed nights for your patrons?

• Would it be possible for you to play on your sound system a tape I've created for recreational purposes? It begins with the famous countdown ('5, 4, 3, 2, 1'). Then I cry 'Thunderbirds Are Go!' followed by the theme music overdubbed with my wife's orgasmic groans. I'm told that it works quite well as industrial techno.

STAN MADELEY
THE UK'S TOP RICHARD MADELEY LOOKALIKE
BM NOUMENON, LONDON, WC1N 3XX   EMAIL: STAN@STANMADELEY.COM

• Finally, would it be possible to hire a private room where we might enjoy other forms of puppetry?

I trust that you can answer these questions and I hope that you don't feel that I've overstepped the bounds of decency. After all, what is the world but a wonderfully variegated panorama of tastes and delights? We shouldn't have to apologise for our little quirks and petty armadillos.

I look forward to your reply and thank you for your time.

       Launch tubes active!

       Captain Stanley 'Thunderbird 1' Madeley

STAN MADELEY
THE UK'S TOP RICHARD MADELEY LOOKALIKE
BM NOUMENON, LONDON, WC1N 3XX EMAIL: STAN@STANMADELEY.COM

Torture Garden
TG Productions Ltd
111 Cremer Business Centre
37 Cremer St
London, E2 8HD

29th November, 2009

Dear Fellow Fetishists,

Hello again. You might remember me. The name is Stanley Madeley (by deed poll) and I'm the UK's top Richard Madeley lookalike. I wrote to you some time ago requesting information regarding my requirements as one of the UK's most imaginative advocates of rubberised Thunderbirds gear.

I have waited some months now for your reply and have still not received it. Yet on the World Wide Web your very own Mistress Charlotte TG wrote: '[I] would like Stan Madeley to identify him/herself so I can congratulate them on the best letter we've received in years'. Well, here I am wearing my crotchless Virgil Tracy outfit, fully identified, yet still awaiting your response to the best letter you've had in years.

Your silence baffles me. My wife had told me to bide my time, but it has now become frustrating. In fact, it has become so frustrating that I finally realise what you're doing: this is the epistolary version of stringing me up by my nipples and slapping me on my behind with a moulting dwarf! Bravo, you clever torturers, you! I consider myself satisfied with your punishment and would now like a considered response to my ideas.

It's getting paramount that my wife and I move our activities to larger premises. Last Tuesday night, Sandra (54) was hanging from the rig when she flew into the bedroom from the landing. Her green latex Thunderbird 2 outfit looked quite spectacular as she used a couple of small kitchen fire extinguishers as thrust jets to slow her down. However, just as she was making her final approach, the ceiling bracket snapped, sending her spinning out of control into the wardrobe. Friday morning, the man from the council informed us that these ceilings weren't made for suspending women of my wife's ample girth dressed as Thunderbird 2. I agree. A small terraced house is just too small for such a spectacle. We really need the space of the Torture Garden to enjoy our role play.

Sandra suggests that I might need to be more masterful with you since it's the only language you understand. Well . . . pull your fingers out of whatever holes they are prodding and do me the courtesy of replying. That's right. Kiss the boot! You know that I've got it. Oh yes. I'll make you beg. Beg me. Come on. You are all dirty minxes and I need to be firm with you. This is me being firm. Taste the leather. You are all my puppets and I wiggle my fingers thusly and you dance. Dance for me my marionettes! Dance and write me a reply! I command thee!

I remain, your most humble servant,

Stanley Madeley

What kind of world is this when you can't even arrange to perform lewd acts in front of strangers?

HELP!!! MY LIP IS STUCK IN MY ZIP...

STAN MADELEY
THE UK'S TOP RICHARD MADELEY LOOKALIKE
BM NOUMENON, LONDON, WC1N 3XX   EMAIL: STAN@STANMADELEY.COM

Ms. Selina Scott   7th October, 2009
Selina Scott Socks,
Pasture House Brookside
Hovingham
North Yorkshire, YO62 4LG

Dear Selina,

Allow me to introduce myself. My name is Stanley Madeley (by deed poll) and, as you can see, I am the UK's top Richard Madeley lookalike, currently touring with my hit cabaret road show, 'Soap Showered Suffragette – The Stanley Madeley Experience Live!'. I was recently in North Yorkshire so perhaps you caught the show. If you didn't, it's no problem. I am not writing with regard to my cabaret career, successful though it is. I'm writing as one land-owner to another who shares a passion for quality ankle-wear.

You see, my wife and I have a few acres of land up in Scotland where Sandra (wife, 54) enjoys making her own synthetic fibres. She has recently started to produce her own high quality environmentally aware spandex (she calls it 'Sandrex') from renewable resources. With her eye for design, she is producing some simply stunning material. Since wife and self are such long-time fans of your products (and, personally speaking, your stunning TV shows), we wondered if you'd be interested in incorporating our spandex into your socks. There's a polka dot design that would be perfect for the woman on the go, and, indeed, my wife has designed most of her fabrics for the semi-serious sports market.

With my flair for creative thinking, I thought we could market them as Selina Scott's Select Self-Supporting Severely-Spotted Sustainable Scottish Spandex Speciality Semi-Serious Sports Socks, or SSSSSSSSSSSSSSS for short. The beauty of the SSSSSSSSSSSSSSS design is that it combines your love for traditional fibres with some of the hardest wearing heal gussets in the business. And, as you can see, it also has an immediately recognisable brand name. Imagine a baseball hat with SSSSSSSSSSSSSSS across the front (and perhaps around to the side). You can't buy marking knowhow like that, Selina. Nike would go purple if they caught a whiff of your socks.

My wife is extremely excited by SSSSSSSSSSSSSSS and even spent Saturday and Sunday suggesting to some sojourning soldiers and sailors that SSSSSSSSSSSSSSS shows signs of being a simply splendid success! I would personally like your permission, Selina, to trademark SSSSSSSSSSSSSSS and rescue the domain name, www.sssssssssssssss.com from the current owners, the South Sussex Socialist Society of Somewhat Sadistic Sadists and Seriously Strange Sodomites. I've made initial contact with them regarding the address, though their demands are a little out of the ordinary. I might have to buy new underwear before we move forward on that front (or, indeed, behind).

Anyway, tell me what you think. To be honest, I'm full of ideas almost as good as this one. If we can establish a foothold (pun intended) with SSSSSSSSSSSSSSS, I would like us to go on and

STAN MADELEY
THE UK'S TOP RICHARD MADELEY LOOKALIKE
BM NOUMENON, LONDON, WC1N 3XX   EMAIL: STAN@STANMADELEY.COM

capture the market for scarves, with Selina Scott's Seriously Sinuous Sumptuously Stitched Stretchily Snug Striped Stylish Scarves. However, I credit you with being a perceptive woman, Selina, so I'll say no more about future products before you spot the tricks of my marketing genius.

I will end by simply thanking you so much for your time and express how much I look forward to hearing your opinion of what is sure to be a hugely successful range of socks, scarves, smalls and sundries.

Signing self sincerely,

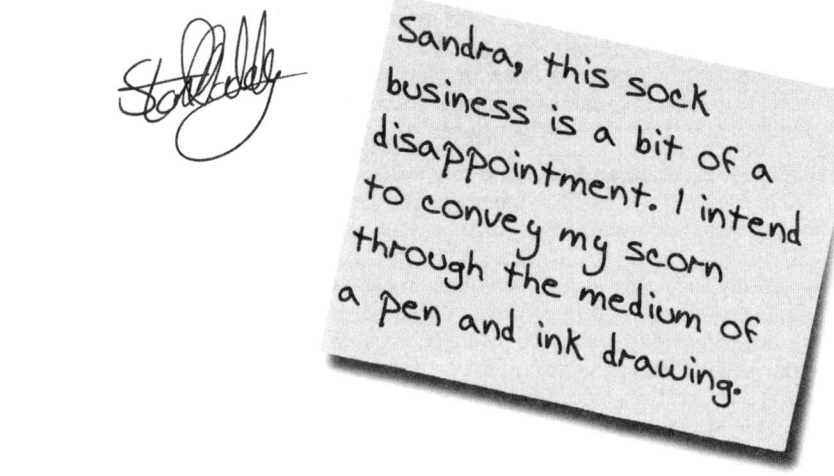

Sandra, this sock business is a bit of a disappointment. I intend to convey my scorn through the medium of a pen and ink drawing.

Jeremy? Is that you? What on earth has Selina talked you into this time?

STAN MADELEY
THE UK'S TOP RICHARD MADELEY LOOKALIKE
BM NOUMENON, LONDON, WC1N 3XX   EMAIL: STAN@STANMADELEY.COM

The Ergonomics Society
Elms Court
Loughborough
LE11 1RG

3rd September, 2009

Dear Sir/Madam,

Allow me to quickly and 'ergonomically' introduce myself. Name's Stanley Madeley (by deed poll) and I'm the UK's top Richard Madeley lookalike, professional bassoonist, and cabaret act.

I bet you're wondering why I'm writing to you good people at The Ergonomics Society. Well, let's be ergonomic about it and cut the flim flam: I am an enthusiastic ergonomicist with something of a knack for spotting design flaws. I have recently written to British Rail to suggest they move the door buttons on their trains down by an inch, to put them in line with the average passenger's elbow. I have also patented my design for a new type of steam iron whose handle is set 45 degrees to the body so it doesn't strain the arm when turning along a particularly proud gusset or seam. I have patented designs for an adjustable hem system for trousers (see illustration), bingo markers for knitting enthusiasts (see other illustration), self-lubricating ball bearing, an organic spark plug, and a special type of garden fork with asymmetrical prongs (and I'm sure I needn't explain how important that is!).

Since I am financially independent thanks to the profits of my newest invention, an electronic butter duck, which always deposits the right amount of butter on your toast, I am looking for unpaid work in a sector I enjoy. Could you tell me if there is any position in The Ergonomics Society for a Richard Madeley lookalike and semi-professional ergonomicist? Just in terms of public profile, I'm sure I could provide a great boost to the science of ergonomics. I am willing to appear in public service broadcasts or help promote the Society through personal appearances.

I thank you for your time and eagerly look forward to your reply. And you might like to know that this letter is printed on a specially adapted ink jet printer fitted with a cartridge containing my own formula of ink made from 20% prune juice.

I defy you to lick this page and say it doesn't taste of prune!

Ergonomically yours,

[signature]

Leg

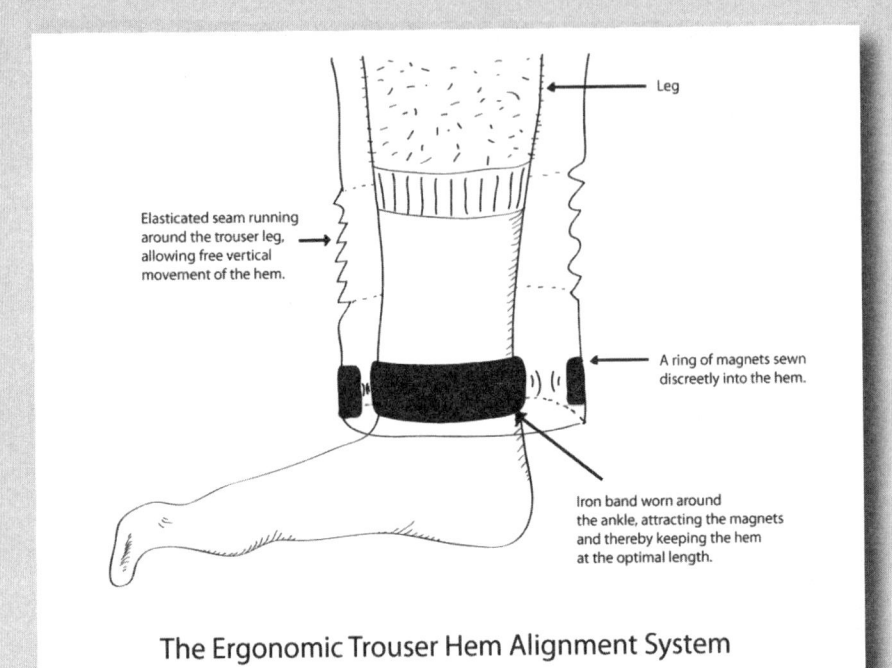

Elasticated seam running around the trouser leg, allowing free vertical movement of the hem.

A ring of magnets sewn discreetly into the hem.

Iron band worn around the ankle, attracting the magnets and thereby keeping the hem at the optimal length.

The Ergonomic Trouser Hem Alignment System

Bingo Elbow Dabbers

The Ergonomics Society
Elms Court
Elms Grove
Loughborough
Leicestershire LE11 1RG

telephone +44 (0)1509 234904
fax +44 (0)1509 235666
email ergsoc@ergonomics.org.uk
web site www.ergonomics.org.uk

Celebrating 60 years of ergonomics

The Ergonomics society

Stanley Madeley
B M Noumenon
London WC1N 3XX

15 September 2009

Dear Stanley

Thank you for your letter of 3 September expressing an interest in the Society. I am enclosing an application form for Associate Membership as I'm sure you would benefit from joining us.

I have passed your information on to Tina Worthy, our Newsletter Editor, who I'm sure would be interested in publicising your achievements to our readership. If you would like to submit anything, please send it me at the Society address above. Also, if you would like to participate in our Annual Conference next April, please visit the website for details (www.ergonomics.org.uk).

I look forward to hearing from you.

Yours sincerely

D H O'Neill
Chief Executive

Enc

Chief Executive
Dave O'Neill
President
Tom Stewart
Honorary General Treasurer
Mic Porter

Company limited by guarantee V.A.T No. 716 4073 48
Registered in England no 1923559 Charity no 292401
Registered office: Elms Court, Elms Grove
Loughborough, Leicestershire LE11 1RG, UK

STAN MADELEY
THE UK'S TOP RICHARD MADELEY LOOKALIKE
BM NOUMENON, LONDON, WC1N 3XX   EMAIL: STAN@STANMADELEY.COM

Mr. Bamber Gascoigne   22nd February, 2010
Chairman
HistoryWorld
92 Highgate Hill
London, N6 5HE

Dear Bamber,

Long-time fan, first-time caller: allow me to introduce myself. The name is Stanley Madeley (by deed poll) and I'm a professional showman with particular interest and involvement in the world of cabaret. I am writing because I've spent the last nine months travelling the UK performing a novelty act inspired by (but not copied from) your own work on the HistoryWorld website (http://www.historyworld.net/). Allow me to add that HistoryWorld is a fantastic resource which I never fail to commend to my audiences. Your 'potted' history of pottery and porcelain hasn't been bettered!

My show takes old-fashioned variety skills and injects them into an interactive learning environment, whilst the fact that I'm also the UK's top Richard Madeley lookalike doesn't harm the operation either. My previous tour about the world's greatest plagues was also highly acclaimed and drew impressive box office receipts. However, critics have repeatedly remarked that I am not always confident with the material, especially some of the foreign words. Certainly, whilst I'm blessed by an abundance of cabaret knowhow and good looks, I am lacking a certain intellectual weight. To be perfectly honest, Bamber: I'm not as bright as you. However, if you don't mind my saying, whilst you are blessed by an abundance of intellectual weight and good looks, you are lacking cabaret knowhow. Herein, I believe, we have a perfect opportunity for some symbiosis (from the Greek word meaning, 'you scratch my back, I'll scratch yours'.)

Much as I love your approach to education, I think you need to reach out to audiences who might not be naturally drawn to history when it's written on the page. So here's my idea, straight out of left field: have you thought of moving into stock car racing?

My brother-in-law Don is a pretty big name in banger racing and he's offered to set us up with a two-seat Vauxhall Corsa. I propose that we rig out the car with a powerful Tannoy system. I'll drive whilst you narrate history to a destruction derby audience who normally wouldn't care a hoot about Zoroastrianism, as fascinating as it is. You will be fully strapped in and wearing a helmet so safe at all times. You can keep your notes (as if you'd need them!) on your lap, though there would also be a fire extinguisher between your knees for emergencies. It's a twenty-five lap race or the last car rolling. I have high hopes of finishing in the top ten, which means a good twenty minutes of driving the oval, taking the bone crunching impacts from the other cars, and proselytising to the untutored many as to the significance of iron to the Hittites. I'm sure you'll view this offer with a little cynicism but I'm very much committed

STAN MADELEY
THE UK'S TOP RICHARD MADELEY LOOKALIKE
BM NOUMENON, LONDON, WC1N 3XX EMAIL: STAN@STANMADELEY.COM

to taking education to the masses, even if those masses are to be found at a car rally on a Wednesday night in rainy Dagenham.

Can I end by saying how much I've enjoyed your books over the years? Your *Brief History of the Great Moguls* was a corker and I don't travel without my copy of *How to Identify Prints: A Complete Guide to Manual and Mechanical Processes from Woodcut to Inkjet*.

Hope you like the stock car idea and I look forward to sharing many rear-end shunts in your company.

Your friend in cabaret,

English translation:

My apologies for late reply: due to a muddle in the office your letter has only just reached me. Your vision of us both rattling around the Dagenham circuit in an old banger accompanied by amplified history is positively apocalyptic – but, as you will probably not be surprised to hear, is not quite my kind of entertainment. Good luck with all your projects.

Bamber.

STAN MADELEY
THE UK'S TOP RICHARD MADELEY LOOKALIKE
BM NOUMENON, LONDON, WC1N 3XX   EMAIL: STAN@STANMADELEY.COM

Fiona Bruce
The Six O'Clock News
Television Centre
Wood Lane
London, W12 7RJ

3rd November, 2009

Dear Fiona,

Allow me to make the introductions. The name is Stanley Madeley (by deed poll) and I'm the UK's top Richard Madeley lookalike, currently entertaining the troops with my one-man show, 'Look No Top! – The Stanley Madeley Experience Live!'.

Might I begin by saying that, in this house and within earshot of me, you are rarely described as anything other than 'The Lovely Fiona Bruce'. Ah, Fiona! If only the BBC had as many newsreaders with your eyes, they would put the Six O'Clock News right in the middle of the peak schedule, such would be the demand to watch it. Sadly, they don't. Primarily because the BBC have a few too many presenters who look like Huw Edwards, so the idea is clearly a non-starter. However, I'm not writing to talk TV schedules but bend your perfect ear (the right one) about something much more palatable to the British public than Mr. Edwards.

As you might be aware, Ms. Selina Scott has recently launched her own range of knitted sock. I was wondering if you've thought about moving into a similar venture. However, before you dismiss the idea, let me quickly say that I would never suggest something as ordinary as socks to you. Quality socks they may be, but they are still very much socks. Ms. Scott's business is also heavily reliant on sheep. Some might say over-reliant and I would certainly be one of those people. You can't guarantee sheep, Fiona, no matter how many promises they make to you or contracts they sign.

Luckily for you, sheep are not part of my plans. My dear wife, Sandra (54), owns and runs a small machine-tools workshop in Worksop and we would love to have the chance to launch a Fiona Bruce themed angle grinder. Have you ever worked sheet metal, Fiona? I'm sure you would love it. With your face on the box, I think a range of luxury tools would be profitable all the year round. We were thinking of launching with the aforementioned angle grinder, following up with a belt sander, nail gun, and a powerful arc welding kit.

You would be under no obligation to climb ladders, do any kind of heavy duty industrial welding or even grind metal (unless, of course, you wanted to!). You don't even have to agree to use the tools in your own workshop/garage/shed. You would simply be the friendly face who promises that the tools are the very best in the business, no refunds given, void where prohibited by law, should only be used when wearing safety goggles, not suitable for minors under the age of nine years, and may ignite if connected to a power source.

STAN MADELEY
THE UK'S TOP RICHARD MADELEY LOOKALIKE
BM NOUMENON, LONDON, WC1N 3XX   EMAIL: STAN@STANMADELEY.COM

Sandra (54) has knocked together a few sample angle grinders and I'd be happy to have one delivered to you at BBC Centre. On the luxury model, we've gone for a knitted handle, which is better for the sweat and also matches the simply stunning top you wore when reading the news a fortnight last Tuesday.

Would love to hear what you think about the idea. We are big fans of the job you're doing on the *Antiques Roadshow*. If the angle grinder idea doesn't take your fancy, perhaps you'd be interested in some part-time work in cabaret. My show runs three nights a week and I require a new assistant for a variety of tricks. Unlike my old assistant, you have small ears so I foresee no problems with the chisel throwing routine.

Sincerely yours,

Why do you think it is, Sandra, that whenever you ask a celebrity a question, they always send you their photo?

STAN MADELEY
THE UK'S TOP RICHARD MADELEY LOOKALIKE
BM NOUMENON, LONDON, WC1N 3XX   EMAIL: STAN@STANMADELEY.COM

Gilbert & George
████████████
████████████
████████

5th September, 2009

Dear George and dear Gilbert (I will not be constrained by any artificial rules about the order of your names!)

Excuse the intrusion and allow me to introduce myself. My name is Stanley Madeley (by deed poll) and I am the UK's top Richard Madeley lookalike and a fellow artisan working in London, though, to be honest, I often feel like some damn vagabond at your exquisitely leathered heels! You gentlemen have changed my life, and, to a lesser extent, the life of my good wife, Sandra (54). With your permission, I will take time to explain.

Rather naively, I made the typical start of an aspiring enfant terrible by quitting my job as a leisure consultant, divorcing my wife, and marrying a midget. My ex-wife disapproved of the marriage, though quickly struck up a friendship with little Pierre. The three of us were lying in bed one night (walnuts were involved) when I realised that this marriage was so predictable as to be positively reactionary! Naturally, I tried to smear the little fellow in my excrement and post him to the Polish Prime Minister but I found even that idea rather passé, if you catch my drift. Well, the whole thing turned rather ugly and the divorce settlement was overly generous to my nanus. However, what is art if it's not a learning process?

There then followed a rather regrettable period when I was influenced by Jeff Koons and I put my wife on display in a variety of explicit poses. Sadly, during one particularly gruelling afternoon's work when I was trying to suspend her from a light-fitting by a large brass ring attached to her buttocks, the light-fitting broke and my wife fell twenty-seven feet to the ground. Sadly, the vegetable strainer didn't protect her head and the resulting injuries left her in a coma. I spent the next two years nursing her. Yet fear not! The good news is that she came around in July and, ever since, she has been communicating with me on a daily basis via breathing tubes and blinks. And I'm sure it will bring a tear to your eye, Mr. Gilbert (you too Mr. George), when I tell you that the old girl still wants to 'give it a go'.

All new artists want to break the taboos and we're no different. Smeared in liposuction fat taken from the arse end of a celebrity trollop, I will be standing naked in the Mall next week, wielding a twenty-seven-inch bratwurst, with which I intend to beat the inert body of wife as she stands (with the aid of suitable support struts) strapped to two snapping turtles aimed towards Buckingham Palace. I calculate the journey up the Mall will take approximately 178 days if I gently paddle her forwards in 12-hour shifts and only stop for bathroom breaks,

STAN MADELEY
THE UK'S TOP RICHARD MADELEY LOOKALIKE
BM NOUMENON, LONDON, WC1N 3XX EMAIL: STAN@STANMADELEY.COM

TV interviews, and to change the turtles. I think this performance art will say all that needs to be said about sex, disability, race, the environment, celebrity and politics and will be as good as anything I've seen on the Fourth Plinth. (Hang your head in shame, Gormley!)

Which brings me to my reason for writing: I can't come up with a suitable title for the piece. My wife suggested (after much puffing of her tube) 'Louisiana lung mustard'. I feel it's too specific and wondered if you could suggest a title. I have included a signed glossy as our gift to thee.

Your friend in performance art,

I don't think they bought it, Sandra. We'll go to Plan B: our very own arts centre built as a giant replica of Ashley Cole's underpants.

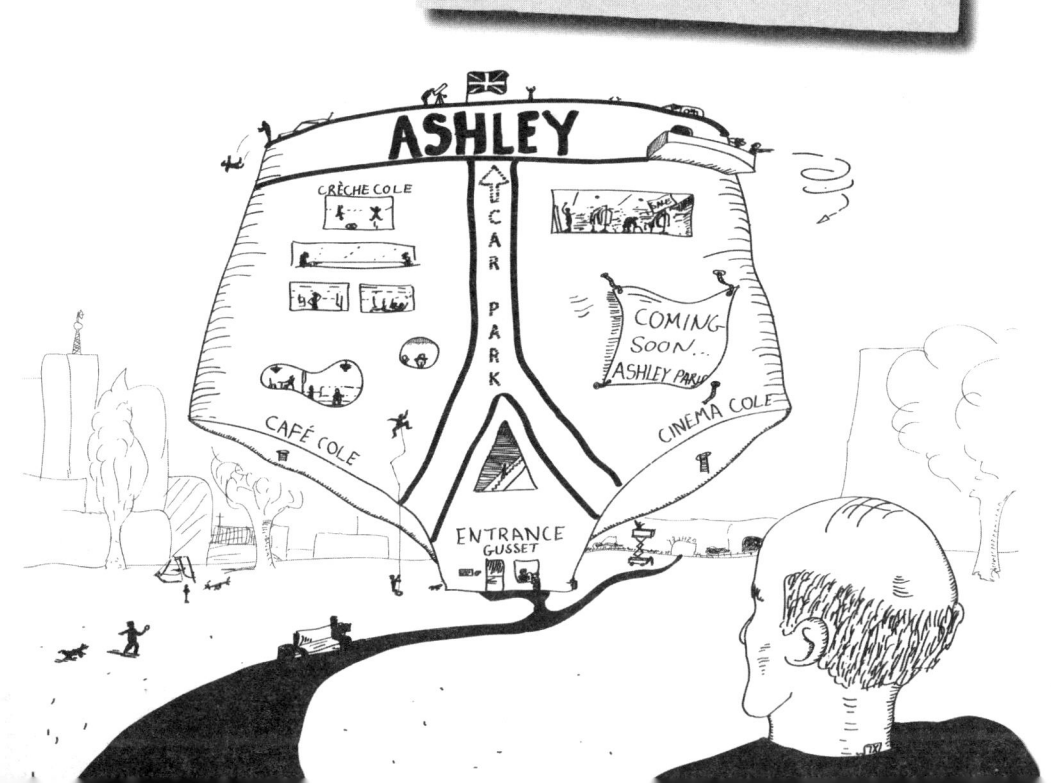

```
S   T   A   N           M   A
THE  UK'S  TOP  RICHARD  MA
BM NOUMENON, LONDON, WC1N 3XX    EMAI
```

> *Notice the lack of a reply, Sandra? I've told you before. I command respect. These SAS types know not to mess with me!*

Andy McNab
c/o Lucas Alexander Whitley Ltd
14 Vernon Street
London W14 0RJ

Dear Andy,

Allow me to introduce myself. My name in Stanley Madeley (by deed poll) and, as you might know, I am the multi-award-winning Richard Madeley lookalike working out of cabaret in Central London.

I'm not writing to pick a fight but, in many ways, I am. You see, I have two reasons for complaint. I recently bought a signed copy of your latest 'novel', which I was intending to present to my wife on the occasion of her 62nd birthday. She's a big fan of your work, having served 14 years in the Territorial SAS. The signed book was going to be her main gift, so you can perhaps appreciate my disappointment when I opened it to discover the following written on the front page.

[signature]

I don't mean to sound impertinent but do you make a regular habit of signing your books 'Andy Nob'? And do you think it's the sort of thing that a married man should be giving to his wife on her birthday? Now, before you get angry, I'm sure you're handy with your fists but I haven't become the nation's top Richard Madeley lookalike without learning a few tricks of my own. When I realised what a cruel hoax you'd played on my wife, I immediately had a thought to box your ears.

On a second and more personal note, I've noticed on your website and elsewhere that you keep talking about 'The Stan'. Now, you might think that you're referring to Afghanistan but, to the majority of your audience, they will think of 'The Stan', the well-known cabaret singer and harp soloist. I have traded under that name for a number of years and would be grateful if you'd stop encouraging the government to send more troops my way.

However, as I said, I'm not here to pick a fight, though you need only mention a time and place and I'll be there. What I do expect is that you start to show a little respect for your audience. You don't want to rile me, sir, lest you get the same treatment I gave Jilly Cooper when it looked like she'd signed her book 'Jockie Cocky', which happens to be another of my nicknames.

Think on, sir. Think on! You wouldn't wish me to warn you again. I've included a signed copy of my most recent glossy so you have an idea of my physical condition and structural weak points.

Sincerely yours,

[signature]

Stanley 'The Stan' Madeley (Pugilist)

STAN MADELEY
THE UK'S TOP RICHARD MADELEY LOOKALIKE
BM NOUMENON, LONDON, WC1N 3XX   EMAIL: STAN@STANMADELEY.COM

Mr. Santa Claus
Santa's Grotto,
Reindeerland,
SAN TA1

27th November, 2009

Dear Santa,

At this point, I would normally wish you well as another festive season approaches. However, at the risk of sounding like a party pooper: I can do without your bloody 'ho, ho, ho'-ing this year and find your presence on our high streets, TV screens, and rooftops a proper imposition. If you think I'm climbing up to make sure our shingle is safe for your landing, you've another thing coming. Why don't you just clear off before you break your neck, you silly old goat? For me, you can cancel Christmas. Let's move straight into January and we'll save on the tinsel.

To start with: I don't want to have friends around. I can do without those last minute trips to the off-licence to see some bleached blonde tart the shape of a turnip dressed in a tinsel sash dress and holly trimmed hat trying to disguise the fact that she has an enormous arse and the personality of a North Korean cabinet meeting.

I also refuse to mimic the Americans by competing to see who can drape more electrically unsound strings of lights around their gutters to strangle the wildlife and put 240 volts down the drainpipe. And leaving your external decorations up for twelve months does not constitute making an effort when all you have to do is connect a two-way on December 1. Santa, there's a simple rule of thumb: if the house is brighter than Heathrow's Terminal One, you're going to find a thong hanging over the fireplace and a stone drunk mother in slate grey sweatpants lying in the chimney place, her arse antler tattoo welcoming you with a festive message written in Chinese ideograms, though 'idiot-grams' is more likely but no doubt Mrs. Claus has one too.

People simply take Christmas for granted. Barclaycard can see us coming! Too much food, alcoholic consumption through the roof or at least down the sink in the kitchen at 3.30 in the morning after eating a Christ-knows-what-it-was-it-looked-like-chicken-biryani-but-tasted-like-prawny... I mean: Jesus! You wouldn't know it's a religious holiday. Not that we're meant to mention the fact in case we upset the Buddhists. It's all a load of old cobblers anyway. What are the Buddhists going to do? Come back at us as a moth? And who wants to be tolerant and full of compassion at Christmas? We need to be armed to the teeth and ready to take anybody out at the ankles for even coming near us with a sprig of mistletoe. Mistletoe: the get out of jail card for sexual deviants everywhere.

Now, I don't want you to think I'm a misanthropist when my only crime is disliking people in general and individually too, but who really deserves a present this year? I was at the dentist today and the woman across from me couldn't stop scratching her arse. And she was the hygienist. We just haven't been good girls and boys this

STAN MADELEY
THE UK'S TOP RICHARD MADELEY LOOKALIKE
BM NOUMENON, LONDON, WC1N 3XX   EMAIL: STAN@STANMADELEY.COM

year. We've done nothing but infect each other with swine flu. Those of us who have had it are guilty of spreading it; those of us who haven't had it are merely waiting to provide a suitable host when the damn thing mutates and starts to eat through steel. Speaking of which: where is Superman when you need him? I'll tell you: stuck behind razor wire in the Fortress of Solitude playing Call of Duty and ordering Domino's Pizzas.

And do you really want to reward a country whose greatest artistic achievement is standing on a plinth in Trafalgar Square? And Simon Cowell has still not been hit by a flesh-eating bug so you clearly gave bugger-all consideration to the Christmas list I sent you last year. And what does the New Year have in store for us? More viruses and Esther Rantzen running for political office!

I sometimes wonder if I'd not be better off as a moth.

       Looking forward to Easter!

Stan Madeley hopes you have A VERY MERRY CHRISTMAS!
Because if the North Koreans don't get us in the New Year, the Iranians will!

Afterword by Mrs Sandra Madeley (54)

When my husband Stanley asked me to write this afterword I reminded him that the last time I closed for him was when I was the busty sister in the Cleethorpes Sisters though I wasn't a real sister and none of us were from Cleethorpes. In them days Stanley used to call me his 'young slip of frilled ginger' which made me chuckle because he always said he was only warming up the crowd before we came out hopping to 'Wake Me Up Before You Pogo' which went on to become a big hit for Wham though they changed the words and didn't do the trick where our sticks got caught in our brassieres and ripped them off. But don't you go thinking it was a classy gig. Oh no! My Stanley didn't start out as the UK's top Richard Madeley lookalike and when I first met him he was smoking forty a day and doing an act called 'Coughs of the Rich and Famous'. I soon put an end to that when he agreed to marry me, but when he asked me to close for him it certainly brought back the memories: the lights, the music, Stan's phlegm bucket. Not that all this talk of showbiz means I'm used to writing words to folk like yourselves with fax machines and fancy prawns and who knows what else made from plastic. At first I thought Stanley was trying to get on my good side because of what happened with Mrs. Pepper's goldfish but he said he really wanted me to write this afterword so I asked him what he'd like me to say and he told me to be myself, thank you all for reading his book, and not to mention Mrs. Pepper's goldfish . . . So I just want to say that our Stanley worked very hard on this book and he hopes that you enjoyed it, but isn't that typical of my Stanley who's the same considerate loving husband I married at the top of Blackpool Tower all those years ago when he stamped that seagull to death after it tried to eat the plastic plumbs off my wedding dress. Now me, I don't put up with no nonsense and I tell him, Look at her at number 89 – she always sees the good in people and that's how she's ended up with four kids by five different fathers and the name of a gas fitter tattooed above her knickers.' Most people don't have any class except Quentin at the *Daily Mail*, proper gent what with him saying things like 'corker' and 'I chuffing well think so' and he'd never have a name tattooed over his backside, but if he does I hope it's mine. There's one thing they say about Sandra Madeley and it's that I'm a firm believer in treating people like they treat you. The other day I was standing outside Wilko's, by the art stall selling those gorgeous 3-D pictures – 'lenticular' Stanley tells me to call them because I'm a serious collector – looking at some Last Suppers, just like the real thing except Jesus now waves to you when you move your head. I think all the Old Masters should be done that way on account of Jesus looking like somebody who did quite a bit of waving but that's probably because he looks like Richard Branson only I can't see God having teeth like that. So you might say I believe in God just not a toothy god . . . Anyway, who do I see but Doreen Pepper who tells me she's been in hospital for new hips and is now off to give them a run out around Australia so I said of course we'd be happy to look after the house because that's what a good neighbour does, though not everybody is that considerate are they? Jeremy Paxman didn't reply to Stanley's letters and that was after I missed Sunday night bingo to watch his rubbish series about Victorian painters who didn't even know the meaning of lenticular and as for that Clive James he just broke my Stanley's heart . . . Anyway, it's a good job that our Stanley was stubborn enough to keep writing his letters otherwise this book might never have got written and it's like I said to him the other night, 'You can keep yanking that chain until you're blue in the face, Stanley Madeley, but it isn't going to flush down when its swim bladder is full of air.' But that's my husband for you. He wouldn't stop until he'd flushed that goldfish away.

Sandra Madeley (54)
St Helens Theatre Royal
14th July 2010

THE ✦ APOLLO WARRINGTON

A *SPECIAL* FESTIVAL OF THANKS
YOUR MASTER OF CEREMONIES: MR. STAN MADELEY

MR. JOBY SPRAGG HUNTS THE PICCADILLY MIDGET

TONY WYER — PSYCHIC WALNUTTING

ACTION MUMBLING WITH MR. DAN SHELSTON

MR. DAVID FEENEY
A NIGHT OF PATRIOTIC SONG, FOOTBALL TRIVIA & MIME!

SCEPTICAL BRYAN AND HIS MUSICAL COWBOY BOOTS

COZY & DIPPY THE BILLIARD TWINS

MR. ANDREW NIXON
AND HIS PET WEASEL *HUMPHREY*

THE VENTRILOQUIST POET **LORD BERNARD** AND HIS MANSERVANT BEATTY

THE SUFFOLK MERMAID **MS. SARAH BALE** BALANCES THIMBLES & SPOONS

THE AMAZING H ONE GNOME BAND

ELBERRY RUNE YODELLER

BUTTERFLY JAZZ WITH NIGE

MR. STUART WARWICK EROTIC CONTORTIONIST WITH HIS LOVELY ASSISTANT BABS (CIRCA 1963)

MR. DAVID LEIGHTON'S **MONK LEVITATION** FEATURING BROTHER PEPE AND *THE HARMONITES*

MS. KERRY CHAPPLE UNRAVELS THE MANUSCRIPT FROM HELL

DON CLEGHORN AND HIS WELL-ENGINEERED **TROMBONE**

MS. LINDSAY DAVIES SKATES THROUGH **THE EDITORIAL HOOPS of HORROR!!!**

THE GILL MULLOOLY **SINGERS**

TOASTER TRICKS WITH JO HOLLAND

WITH SPECIAL GUEST STAR **MR. O'MARA AND HIS MIRACLE MOOD TONIC**

PLUS **RON AND EILEEN** DANCE WITH LIONS!

THIS BOOK IS LOVINGLY DEDICATED TO THE MEMORY OF MY FATHER, FRANK.